LITTLE BITES

My Domestic Violence Roadmap to Safety and Peace

Bobbin Aspland

Smillie Publications
VICTORIA, AUSTRALIA

Copyright © 2025 by **Bobbin Aspland**

All rights reserved. Except as permitted under the Australian Copyright Act 1968, no part of this book may be reproduced, stored in a retrieval system, communicated or transmitted in any form or by any means without prior written permission.

**Bobbin Aspland/Smillie Publications
Victoria, Australia**

Publisher's Note: Little Bites, My Domestic Violence Roadmap to Safety and Peace is a true account of the author's life experience. Any information is the author's understanding at the time of writing this memoir. It is shared for the purposes of informing the public of potentialities available to everyone, to heal and transform. While all events are factual, names have been changed to protect a person's identity. This body of work is written and produced by a living natural native being of the Earth and is non-AI.

Book Layout © 2024 BookDesignTemplates.com

Little Bites/Bobbin Aspland. -- 1st ed.
ISBN 978-0-646-70999-4

Dedication

For my children
&
For all women and men and their loved ones who have suffered from the acts of domestic violence

To remove ourselves from fear takes courage, this courage we acquire through refusing to let fear dictate our actions.

AUTHORS NOTE

My story of escaping domestic violence won't be the same as your story. Only through the act of sharing our personal experiences can we support each other, learn and grow together, and rise above these insidious acts of harm against women.

Throughout the pages of Little Bites you will read about the steps I took that helped me move forward, grow in confidence and courage and deepen my compassion for myself and others who have experienced the effects of a toxic relationship. While no pathway clear of abuse is easy to navigate, I found many key areas that have assisted me to thrive.

Our unique journeys are so precious. I invite you not to wait any longer and rewrite your story, from the inside out, and the outside in. As you receive my words and read about my experiences, it is my heart's wish that there be gems that provide you with ideas and support to make the changes necessary to live the life you have dreamed of.

Stay safe. Be kind to yourself. Take little bites.

CONTENTS

PART ONE 1
THE ESCAPE 3
   Non-Lethal Strangulation 13
STAYING SAFE 19
THE TRANSITION 31
SUPPORT 45
   The Rabbit Hole – A Very Dark Place 53
   Little Bites 57
WET FISH MOMENTS 65

PART TWO 81
NAVIGATING OUR WAY 83
MAKING ROOM WITHIN OURSELVES 99
   Narcissist and trauma 100
LAUGH AND SMILE 111
CHANGING OUR OUTLOOK 117
EYES TO THE SOUL 141

PART THREE 151
WEDDING CELEBRATIONS 153
MOVING FORWARD 159
REFLECTION 165

INTRODUCTION

Although the author is not known, the following words resonated with me so much that I wanted to pass it on. My wish is that this metaphor for life inspires all children to recognise the wonders that they are.

As you read through, I'd like you to imagine what your tree of life might look like.

- Become aware of the roots of who you are. Reflect upon how you have been influenced by your family and your early environment. Notice how your roots anchor you to the ground and give you stability.
- Now look at your trunk; see the marks on the bark and notice the scars that you have gathered as you have developed and grown. Are there any wounds that still have not healed?
- See the leaves and the buds that are forming. The buds are your hopes and dreams that will one day come to fruition; nurture them and they will blossom into your future.
- And now look at the fruits of your tree; these are your successes and achievements. Look how colourful and splendid they are. Spend some time appreciating the fruits of your labour.
- Finally, imagine your tree in winter with its bare branches, standing silent and proud. And know that

even in the darkest days your tree is buzzing with inner life as it prepares itself for a new and hopeful spring.
- Admire the strength, vigour, and purpose of your tree.

As women we may marry, if we're fortunate we bring children into the world to raise, nurture, and provide material support, our deepest desire being to ensure a loving life for our children as our love for them is unending. Unfortunately, some women are abused and exploited. Often, after many years of abuse there comes a pivotal point when enough is enough, a trigger is released from within us, we've reached a point where necessity brings about the need to live. I'm not immune to peoples' thoughts 'Why didn't you leave earlier?'

Of course, this is easier said than done. It is one thing to leave such a situation; it is quite another to know where to seek the support systems around you, to take that step, one needs to feel SAFE. Once we have sought safety and have begun the journey of recovery from these traumatic events, we need to allow the space and time for our emotions to set free.

The time we take depends on our individual circumstances and characters. This was a process that didn't take weeks or months for me to navigate; it has taken me years.

Most commonly, women who encounter domestic violence are labelled victims which only adds weight to the hard emotional times ahead. It is understandable that to move forward and find our new lives we must endure deep emotional release yet as each outburst is expressed a magical reset occurs. Adding children to the mix complicates everything!

Before leaving a DV situation it makes sense to rehearse the process of leaving in your mind, plan where you are going to stay, ensure the location is somewhere that you know you will feel safe. Who are the people or contacts that you can rely on to provide you with the emotional support through this time? What financial support will you need? You might be working, sure, but what if he comes to your workplace and creates a scene? Sometimes it is helpful if work colleagues are informed of your circumstances. And if someone flippantly asks, 'Why didn't you just move out?' this is not a criticism of you, it is their inability to walk in your shoes. They do not know what happens behind closed doors.

In the end, I did not have any time to make my plans of where, when, or how I would get out; I simply knew I had to leave. For some, it literally becomes a matter of life or death and the short time frame could be hours or, minutes. Everyone's experience is slightly different. I left when I did because I chose to live and realised living in fear and survival mode was not living.

While I am only one of many who has lived through these traumatic life events, I feel the need to express not solely by what happened to me but by how I managed after leaving, reaching out to others who have been or are going through similar situations.

My purpose for writing this book is to let women who have experienced domestic violence know they are not alone. Every woman who has been subject to the traumas, will eventually have to travel their own unique journey of recovery. There are many books available on this subject matter and it is my hope and wish that my journey may speak to you in ways that I cannot even comprehend. You may find parts of this book useful to you, fantastic, I have achieved my objective. As the various books come to you take from them what you will, there is always something to learn. If you have picked up this book, I can only wish for you a safe and comforting journey. Sure, it will be rough at times but take pleasure in and cherish the little things that come your way, as life does eventually get better.

I found solace in reading not only self-help and spiritual books but books of all sorts. My daughter got me started when I first moved out, she gave me some self-care cards and a lovely journal which I used to capture and contemplate further on what I had read. We each find our own path and garner confidence along the way that is needed to move forward, mine was journalling.

*

While I was journalling, I also kept a scrapbook. My scrapbook contained captions that friends had sent me to keep my spirits up. These lovely sayings provided me with the confidence I needed and often reaffirmed I was on the right track and to keep going. It was when I was updating my scrapbook that I felt the need to start writing, to explain to myself, the changes I was going through.

I shared what I had written with my counsellor and continually said I wanted to write about my journey free, in hopes of helping others. In acknowledgement to the Red Rose Foundation Queensland for the help and support they provided me by way of counselling etc, I felt it important to capture their mission statement called 'Change the Ending.'

I thought my scrapbook was finished, but then new people entered my life, which took me on another journey, a jour-

ney of learning to be stronger and self-reliant, where victimhood and rabbit holes became a distant memory.

I had to learn to say no and set the boundaries - my boundaries, and what that entails. I had to acknowledge that everyone has feelings and when someone stepped beyond my boundaries then it was okay to let them know in a kind and respectful manner. Learning to stand up for myself, after not being able to do that for so many years was a definite balancing act.

Every day, I grow stronger. Life challenges me and I rise to meet those challenges. I recognise I am coping better.

<u>*Big girls shoes on now.*</u>

My favourite saying 'This is an interesting journey!' keeps me open; the trick, I think, is found in my own unique flow. Yes, some things trigger me and make me cry, but from that I learn how to cope better, learn from it and grow stronger.

My determination to keep moving forward provides me with strength, along with my counsellor and friends, both old and new I cherish them all.

I'm changing the ending, and although scary it feels good.

The above is one of my first attempts at capturing my personal inner feelings. I felt so privileged when the Red Rose Foundation Queensland contacted me to ask if they could put this up on their social media page.

The Red Rose Foundation, Queensland, provides services to address domestic violence. Their aim, as outlined on their website, is to eliminate domestic family violence related deaths.1

It was the Strangulation Trauma Centre of the Red Rose Foundation that supported and helped me through my journey.

The Strangulation Trauma Centre of the Red Rose Foundation provides these services:

- Trauma-informed and compassion focused counselling
- Therapeutic groups for women who are survivors of strangulation and high-risk violence.
- A facilitated online group for women
- Individual counselling sessions
- Safety planning
- Telephone support
- Court support and assistance with strangulation matters in the Magistrate and District Court (Brisbane City Courts).
- Support to access ongoing health services
- Systems advocacy

In the first chapter I have alluded to a few instances that occurred to enable you, the reader, to understand some of the events that took place in my life prior to escaping. But I cannot and will not go through all the details and events, it is too raw, besides that would be another book.

My purpose is not to dwell on what has happened in the past, but that this book benefits others on their respective journeys **out** of a DV relationship, and to give possible avenues for moving forward with their respective lives. By sharing my journey, I hope I can shed light and offer hope to those who have experienced or are experiencing similar events.

There are times throughout the book where I have repeated phrases; this is for the purpose of reassurance and focused attention to maintain a positive outlook.

For the purpose of my retelling of the events, I shall refer to my ex-husband as He, 'He who shall be obeyed.'

We grow from having dared to live.

PART ONE

It's important to acknowledge and understand that by overcoming some of the harsh realities of life, of the dangers and challenges we face, we grow. We gain strength in our actions and through our determination.

CHAPTER ONE

THE ESCAPE

'You had better leave; I'm getting angry and I will be angry for the next few days.'

This was the first time **ever** that I had any warning that the abuse would be coming. Whether it would be verbal or physical, I was never sure. I could never predict; all I knew was that it came in cycles and I had to be prepared. Well, He did not have to tell me twice. From not getting any warning that a push or throw would come, to being told was worrying. My biggest fear was that he was going to strangle me again, as I no longer had anyone living at home who could step in to save me. I knew I had to leave, and leave now.

I learnt over the years how to duck or look away. I tried to avoid being thrown/pushed around to get away from the verbal abuse. Dropping my head in shame and avoiding the death stares became second nature.

On that day I quickly went to the bedroom and sent a text to my daughter-in-law (Annie) asking if she was home and could I come and stay. Annie had visited a few times over the previous weeks. Annie and my son James could see only small glimpses of what was happening, or so Annie had alluded, asking me how could I keep going (with the control and manipulation they could see He exerted over me). Annie told me they always had a place for me to stay if I needed to get away. Now I needed that safe place. She replied to my text: they were home and I was welcome to come over.

I threw a few items into a bag, a few clothes and a wash bag. I was shaking, scared He would come in and start verbally abusing me again calling me everything under the sun; yelling at me about how useless I was, that I used to be pretty but now I had so many wrinkles and looked old and unattractive and overweight that I was shit. Or He would start pushing me around. I had to be quick. I had to get out and away.

I took off in the car as fast as I could. Shaking physically from the threat and thoughts of what could have been, I tried not to think of anything except getting to James and Annie's place in the city suburbs. It was a forty-five-minute drive, enough time to get myself together and stop shaking.

The two grandchildren were there to greet me, with big hugs which was so comforting. I have always loved hugs.

We all said our hellos. As a family, we always greeted each other with a kiss and a hug hello and did the same whenever we were leaving - a kiss and a hug goodbye.

The boys then went into the lounge room to watch some television while I talked with James and Annie out on the back deck, explaining what had happened. They could see I was upset and did not want the boys to hear.

I told them that He and I had been talking of selling off all our furniture and belongings we no longer used for some time now, and they were aware of this. We had accumulated so much 'stuff' over the years, it would be good to have a clean out prior to selling the house and property.

Over the previous months I had spent considerable time researching properties around the Mid Coast that we could potentially move to. I would keep Him up to date on what the property prices were doing, what we could potentially purchase once we sold.

His behaviour towards me had been getting worse over the past few years, but the last few months there had been a real change. He nearly always spent most of the day sleeping in the bedroom; I would be in the kitchen cooking, making sweets, cakes or desserts – double lime cheese cakes, lemon slices or a rolled pavlova. It wasn't so much that I enjoyed eating them, I enjoyed the making of them, and giving them to the kids and grandchildren whenever they came to visit. He never liked me giving them the cakes and desserts. He wanted them for himself, He was not a good one for sharing that way, not unless there was something in it for Him.

I'd be totally engrossed with cooking or baking, and I'd open the fridge door to get ingredients out or place the biscuit base into the fridge to set while I made the cheesecake mix. He would ever so quietly go and stand behind the fridge door, and when I went to shut the door, I would get such a fright. I was always totally unaware that He was there, hidden behind the door. He would laugh. He thought it was so funny to make me scared and frightened. He would do things like this regularly – sneak up behind me, or from behind a door, or the wall of another room – and really scare me.

I begged him to stop, but He would not. He got too much joy out of it. As much as you try to prepare yourself for a fright, you never can. I could not predict when He would suddenly materialise. He always wore socks, so I could never hear his footsteps on the bamboo floor. So much enjoyment he got out of scaring me! This would happen nearly every day, especially after He had had his little lay down. He would laugh his head off.

Our dog, a British Staffordshire terrier named Fred, really was my early warning system and protector. I used to spend my time making bamboo chimes out the back of the house, sitting on the large paved area, something I enjoyed a lot. I liked making the large chimes, usually 1 to 2 meters in length. While I was working on cleaning the bamboo, then preparing it by sanding the bamboo by hand or giving it a clear coat of varnish, or I'd drilling the holes to hang each bamboo piece, He would stand behind the flywire screen inside the house and wait.

I could not see into the house as the screen was dark, black actually, and I couldn't see Him. It was Fred who would stand in front of the flywire screen looking into the house. Fred would bark and continue barking until He fessed up and came out, opening the screen door. Thank goodness for Fred's early warning. It was still a fright, as I was always on tenterhooks. But at least Fred gave me some idea that He was standing there. It softened the shocks a bit.

Fred was always protecting me. Whenever Fred was inside with me and He was outside, walking back to the front door from checking the mail box, Fred would bark. Fred was quite determined in his barking; it was a protective bark, and I was forever appreciative of it.

I suffer from rheumatoid arthritis and had an injury to my leg. Sometime earlier my knee was damaged (due to another DV incident which I shall not go into). Whenever I was sitting on the lounge with my leg up, resting it from the pain, and He came into the lounge from the kitchen, Fred would stand over my legs – Fred's front legs on one side and back legs on the other side of me – and Fred would bark at him. Quite determined to protect me. I always felt safe, but I feared for Fred. He might swing a punch at him. I did believe Fred had his measure though, as he was very quick and agile – and He was never quite sure what Fred might do.

I briefly went over the events of the morning with James and Annie. I was still trying to come to terms with them myself being given a warning, that had never ever happened before.

They said I could stay, although they were concerned as they were really wanting us to sort our differences out, to talk to each other try and find middle ground. I asked if I could stay until my physio appointment which was on Wednesday, six days from now.

I had grown used to the feeling of fear. I had lived in heightened fear for so long, it was only over the previous three years, back home in Queensland, that the feeling of fear became one of needing to survive. The knowing that I might be seriously injured had intensified as his behaviour was escalating, but I could not say anything to anyone. In my thoughts, I was trying to figure out what was worse – was it the physical abuse, or the death stares and verbal abuse, or the controlling? I knew I was going to cop it. The feeling of fear had turned to such a strong feeling of the need to survive.

Going through explaining all this, it does not sound much, but when you are living it, it is a different thing entirely.

In my reading and journalling some considerable time later, I came across brilliant paragraphs. I found it beneficial to learn what we can from the tough lessons and hang on. Enjoy and learn from the journey we are taken on. 'Life is just life;' enjoy choosing the lollies you want.

Fear: - it takes quite a bit of emotional energy to rise above fear and move forward, however once accomplished we prove to ourselves that fear cannot defeat us by doing this, we strip it of its power. Those who WANT us to be afraid try to continuously put us down.

He had chastised me a few weeks earlier for talking too much to my own family, James, Annie, and the grandchildren. We were coming home from visiting them and all the way home in the car, I was abused and rebuked. I was no good, I should not be talking to the kids, I had nothing of value to say, I was shit, I was worthless. I meant nothing to anyone anyway, so I should not talk or communicate. I remained silent all the way home, my head dropped in shame, looking out the passenger window. It really did not warrant saying anything as it would bring on more, and the death stares were horrific.

Each day that I was staying at James's place, He would text consistently, asking me to return home where I belonged, saying that He missed me, I should at home. He phoned Simone (our daughter), telling her she should 'Talk to your mother.' The pressure was being applied.

I did not want to involve the kids; I had always hidden the abuse from the kids and everyone else. My focus in life was to protect my children and bring them up as independent, strong individuals.

He did not have any qualms in using them telling them anything in order to manipulate me. Simone did phone me and asked me to phone all the boys to let them know what had happened. Against my better judgement, I phoned them all. I really didn't want them involved or caught in the middle, and exposed to the events of a dreadful marriage.

The next day I phoned my neighbours. They both worked in the police force, and she was a senior constable working within the domestic violence section of the force. I explained to her what was going on and that I was staying with James for a few days. Her response was quick, she commented that she and her husband had both suspected that He was abusing me, from the way He talked to me. I did not think anyone was picking up on how He was treating me, He was so clever in hiding it or so I thought and I was too scared and ashamed. I explained that I was returning home on the Wednesday after my physio appointment and could we meet for a cuppa and chat on Thursday.

He always portrayed himself as the wonderful partner who looked after me. He would constantly tell everyone how lucky and fortunate I was to have him as my husband. Our life was presented as that happy family.

I would go to work and He would stay home and occasionally cook the evening meals for us when He felt like it. I was the sole breadwinner for the past eleven years. He was the devoted husband – or so he portrayed himself – I should be so grateful that He made me a cup of tea in the mornings; I was so lucky, as He was so good to me. This is the way he always characterised himself to everyone – the devoted, caring husband. It was not worth my while to say anything different; I learned that over the years; the repercussions were not worth it.

When I returned on Wednesday after my physiotherapist appointment, He was sitting at the breakfast bar, I stayed in the kitchen on the opposite side of the bar. He was looking very forlorn and feeling sorry for himself. He kept saying that He could not believe that He did what he did to me years ago, He was referring to the violent rape that happened early in the marriage, in the very late 1970's. It was always his go to, to make me feel so ashamed, his way of putting me into my place, making me feel so disgusted, so humiliated and so worthless. He had the power over me and He wanted me to know it. I would drop my head in shame and disgust, how could anyone treat a person like this with such disdain, what had I done to deserve this?

Shame is a concept few people really understand unless they have experienced it. Some alternative expressions for shame are: being dishonoured, disrespected, disgraced, demeaned, taunted, mocked, subjected to indignity, losing face, being treated as insignificant, and feeling inferior, incomplete, a failure, ugly, unimportant, useless, worthless. Shame is a powerful word that described my feelings of worthlessness well.[2]

I did try to leave years ago following the initial incidents of rape. My employers arranged for me to see a solicitor for advice and gave me the day off to find alternative accommodation which I did. Back in the late 1970's this was unheard of, to have such support, and I am forever grateful.

The first domestic violence awareness was in October 1987, when the first national domestic violence toll-free hotline was established, and domestic violence became a criminal offence in Victoria.3

After I had met with the solicitor and found new accommodation in an apartment half an hour away, I came home from work that day to let Him know I was moving out, and taking the children with me (only two children at that stage). I was not prepared for the onslaught.

I was thrown across the room onto the large wooden dining table and told in no uncertain terms that I would not be taking the children. He was going to keep the children He said, and He'd make sure that they would grow up to hate me. It was made abundantly clear I was not going anywhere.

I had been thrown around before up against cars or against walls, but this really injured my back I could barely move. And so, I stayed. I could not leave my children, I could not risk having Him lose his temper with them, hurting them. I had put myself between the children and Him many a time while they were babies. He would yell out at them loudly, more for my benefit, as they were only babies, 'You want something to cry about, I'll give you something to cry about'. I had to get to them quickly before he started to belt them. I was happy to accept the onslaught of rage if it meant the children were not hurt.

Back home in the kitchen I could hear James's voice in my head asking me to talk it out, 'try and make it work'. I surprised myself finding my voice, and explained it was not only the rape, it was also the time He strangled me, and how the boys had to save me by pulling him off me. I explained that I felt scarred, scared of him. He smiled and walked around to where I was standing on the other side of the breakfast bar.

Stood over me with his hands on his hips puffed his chest out and glared at me saying 'So you're scared of me, are you?' I knew then I had made the biggest mistake in telling him, in trying to be open and tell him how I felt. I had to get out, as it was only a matter of time before I was seriously hurt and there would be no coming back from that one.

In addition to this, I had felt he had been laying some groundwork, planning for something, what I do not know, I was so very fearful. Lately He had been talking about how He had two pieces of tooth left in his gum from when He had tooth extractions while we were living in Victoria. Now back home in Queensland, he had recently visited the local dentist to have one of the pieces of a tooth that was embedded in his gum removed. The next day He was so upbeat and excited. He was a 'changed man.' He was so thrilled He phoned all his brothers and sisters, telling them how his personality had changed. He was back to normal now that he'd had the piece of tooth removed, 'this was so miraculous.' I could not believe what I was hearing.

He went onto explain to them that the piece of tooth that was embedded in his gum was the cause of his terrible tempers and argumentative state. But now He was 'back to normal'. Whatever normal was. But He still had another piece of tooth on the other side which needed to be removed, much like the first one. I asked, even begged him to have the other piece of tooth removed. (If it had changed his personality that much, which of course it had not, but one always lived in hope). I really don't know what his brothers and sisters thought.

He consistently refused to go to the dentist and have the other piece of tooth removed. It was like in his mind He had an excuse for continuing to treat me the way He did, as if the controlling and arguing was only something that had occurred since having the broken piece of tooth in his gums, the verbal and physical abuse, the death stares, the constant put downs, berating me for anything I said or did, well that's how it felt. I was scared.

Non-Lethal Strangulation

The incident of the non-lethal strangulation occurred when we were living on the Sunshine Coast. I was thrown to the floor outside the kitchen next to the breakfast bar. I vividly remember having my knee up against his chest trying to push him off and hold him back having my arms outstretched trying to push him away in an attempt to try and get his hands from around my neck. I remember calling out for help hoping that the neighbours might hear my cries.

I cannot remember if I blacked out or not but I do remember the two boys pulling him off me. Kai took Him into the family room and James took me into the lounge room. I was shaken, the back of my head was hurting from hitting the floor and what I could only describe as being shaken to the core.

Non-lethal strangulation can and did shake me to my core, no matter how late the realisation comes you appreciate you actually have a life that you're not just an object. Life had given me a jolt.

Once in the lounge room, James was crying and begging me to stay, 'All the other kids at school come from broken families, mum. Please don't split up.' He went on and on, begging me to 'please stay together.' What could I do? ... I stayed for my children. Both my younger boys were still at high school.

A few years ago, back at our home in the Gold Coast Hinterland, one of his sisters had moved up from Victoria and had been staying with us for some time until she had established herself on the Sunshine Coast. She would drive down to the hinterland to visit us occasionally. She was witness to his comments towards me, how he would talk at me. She would look at me as if to say, 'Are you really going to take that?' Little did she know what would happen if I didn't.

The past few years when we went grocery shopping, I would be holding onto the trolley and He would walk me into the shelving in the food aisles or push me out of the way when we got to the checkout. I was getting cortisone treatment for the bursitis in the hip and I could not move out of the way quickly enough. I was still going to the physiotherapist to complete exercises to help me cope and move more freely. A few times at the checkout, as he used his body to push me, I felt like I was going to fall.

I remember before we were married, his mother would tell me of his bad temper, that the only way they could settle him down when he was a young child was to turn the garden hose onto him. You would have thought I would catch on. Nope, I was very naïve. I didn't have much self-confidence and had the feeling no one would ever want me, so I took what affection was shown. Narcissists can be very charming.

After the incident of the Wednesday when I returned and attempted to talk through the events of the previous week, and of the years of our marriage, and realised that opening up and explaining how I felt was such a big mistake, I was very keen to get out of the house. I was pleased to be going to the hairdressers on the Thursday, followed by my catch up with the neighbors for a cuppa.

My neighbor and I did not have long; I needed an overview of what to do. What steps should I take to protect myself? I appreciated all her help and advice and returned home before too much suspicion was raised. Although our time was brief, I knew when I got home, He would grill me on what we talked about. And the questions came. I was able to explain that the neighbors had recently sold their property and were moving out in the next week, that we talked about her new home. He seemed to accept that.

But I knew I had to get out.

It was early in the year of 2022 that I escaped. He had a doctor's appointment in the morning. Once he left, I packed a few of my clothes as much as I could into one bag and a wash bag, plus a few other personal items. I was in such a hurry, I felt so panicked, frantic that He might change his mind and come back, not see the doctor at all.

This was a new doctor. Previously, whenever I changed to a different doctor, He would also change to the same doctor I had moved to, insisting He come to my appointments with me. I was so restricted; I could not talk freely. If I insisted, I see the doctor alone, I was grilled afterwards about what was said, what treatment if any I had to have. I had been diagnosed with rheumatoid arthritis a few years earlier, and initially, even when I went for my specialist appointments, He would insist on coming in. Then He would take over the conversation. I had no say, no voice, till I finally found the courage to speak up, explaining I would be fine on my own, 'but thank you for caring.'

I had to feed Fred. As much as I dearly loved Fred, I knew I could not take him. I gave Fred an extra bowl of food and another bowl for water placing them in the ensuite in addition to his normal bowls that were at the other end of the house in the laundry. I showed Fred where they were. Giving him a big hug, I began crying and said I was sorry but I could not take him. I thanked him for his love and protection. This was absolutely gut-wrenching for me.

I waited till I knew He was well out of town; the doctor's surgery was over half an hour away, when I felt it was safe to leave and not be spotted. I drove straight to the police station where I explained that I wanted to make a statement of domestic violence. I asked for the police officer I was advised to reach out to, only to be told she was on leave. I was then made to wait what felt like hours, but it was probably only twenty minutes. I was so very anxious as my car stood out; it was unmissable; it was a very brightly coloured four-wheel drive. The police station was next to the library and the cars parked outside these buildings could be seen from the main car park below where you could access the supermarket and the pharmacy, and a few other shops. I was anxious that He might come back early and spot my car, then come in demanding to know what was going on.

I sat there trying not to cry trying to keep hold of my fear and all the emotions running through me. Finally, I was taken into the interview room, where I went through all the details with the officer. After a while he stopped writing; he had written too many pages in his little notebook, I guess. After that the constable listened, making a few notes here and there. I was becoming increasingly anxious as the time went by. Would He come back and see the car parked outside the police station? I had to go, I had to bolt, I had to get out of town and hide. The officer explained that he would have to contact Him to verify the events, I agreed. How could He deny them, the two boys were witnesses to the strangulation, which happened more than a few years ago now, and they had saved me. The police constable gave me the phone number for DV Connect, and suggested I phone them for support and accommodation. He said he would pass on my information to DV Connect services anyway which I was grateful for. I thanked him and left.

I left upset, not crying, just in turmoil internally. I drove to the nearest major town and parked at the back of some of the shops away from the main thoroughfare, where the car could not easily be seen. Once I felt safe and I had calmed down by doing some deep breathing I started to phone the support numbers I was given for DV Connect.

I kept getting the run around, from one support group to another; it seems jurisdictions relating to different areas came into play. It turned out the only accommodation available for the night in the state was a five-hour drive away, and there was no guarantee that it would still be available when I got there. During one of the phone calls I made, one of the DV support people ask me if I had ever experienced a strangulation. 'Yes,' I replied so they referred me to the Red Rose Foundation Queensland (RRF), giving me their phone number. I thanked her, then phoned RRF, leaving a message.

The police office phoned me back and confirmed that my husband had admitted to everything I had put in my statement. Well, that was a surprise. Throughout our years, He had never ever apologised or said He was sorry for anything. Sorry was not a word in his vocabulary. The officer gave me the report number and advised me he had also contacted DV Connect.

Unbeknown to me, I was to find out about an hour later that the police officer also phoned three of my children. He had not told me he was going to do this. Not long after, the children were phoning me, asking what was going on. The kids wanted to know if I was okay. One of them was working interstate. When he phoned, I assured him I was okay, explaining that there was limited accommodation and I was phoning DV Connect for support, I told him I was happy to spend the night in the car if need be. My other son, James, phoned to find out what the police wanted to talk to him about, as he was tied up in meetings. I briefly explained. Then Simone phoned. 'Mum, what the fuck is going on.'

I told her that I had fled and was going to sleep in the car for the night. She would not have it; I was to meet her at the foreshore on the esplanade after she finished work and I was to stay with her for a while.

Once at her place we sat on the back deck upstairs and I gave her a brief overview of some of the abuse that had happened over the years. Suspicions she had over the years were confirmed for her I felt. At least she was aware of some of it now.

Now, I had escaped.

CHAPTER TWO

STAYING SAFE

Once we emerge from the suffering and our vision has cleared, we begin to feel stronger, our character begins to develop.

The Red Rose Foundation returned my call the next day, and so my support began. This was all so much for me being out away from danger, the relief of not being so afraid all the time. My life was no longer simply surviving from day to day which I had come to realize was not living at all. It all felt so very strange I was not sure what I was feeling. I only knew I was safe for the time being.

The first few weeks were a blur. I was asked what I wanted to do. I did not know, I got out, I was alive and grateful to be so. Everything was different and new, and very scary. What to do? Decisions, Decisions. The best advice I had was from my counsellor at the time warning me that most times when a woman goes back to the partner who abused them, it ends in tragedy.

If I had not had the support of the RRF Queensland, I would not be here today. Their support was invaluable. They listened, talked me through the process. They too explained that many deaths occur when you return to your partner, that people get lonely feel they cannot cope and so return to their partner only to be in a worse situation. I certainly was under no illusions about what the outcome would be if I returned.[1] There was no way I could go back, no matter how hard things got. I knew I had to stay alive, why I do not know.

I felt safe at my daughter Simone's place there were cameras everywhere, out the front and out the back, around the pool and in all the common areas, dining, kitchen, verandas, and hallways. Everywhere except for the bedrooms and bathrooms. He would not come while I was here, as everything would be caught on camera.

And so, my new journey began, finding my feet, being taken along for the ride. I say being taken along for the ride as I had no idea of where to from here or what I was going to do. All I knew for certain was that I wanted to remain safe and alive.

A few weeks later I'd arranged to pick up more of my items from the house clothes etc. It was incredible how people in the 'know', like my counsellor, who have dealt with these situations before could predict exactly what He would say. As He did. He offered to help; He offered this, that and the other. But He wasn't only trying to get me to come back, He wanted to take control of what I was doing.

Counsellors who have helped so many individuals through trauma really do have the knowledge and expertise. When I was feeling like I was struggling they gave me the confidence to continue to remain focused and did not apply any pressure. They were only there to help, unlike other members of my family who wanted to know what I was going to do, what decisions I was going to make. I did not know. What I did know was that I did not want the pressure, I wanted to have time to think and collect my thoughts.

The collection of my clothing plus a few odds and ends I wanted, I needed to do on my own, without any interference from Him. Fortunately, I had the support of Simone and son James in getting the few things I required from the house.

Being concerned for my safety, my counsellor discussed with me all the various scenarios that might occur. Previously my counselor had asked me if He had any weapons in the house. He no longer had the shot gun but did have hunting and flick knives scattered throughout the house. He kept the stick knife in the bedroom, this was a hunting knife with a 250millimeter blade beveled on both sides leading to an extremely sharp point. Not that he ever did any hunting. There was another knife in the study, similar in length but with a serrated edge on one side, then there were the flick and pocket knives throughout. Including the caravan where he kept another flick knife. My counselor was concerned with this information. So we developed numerous contingency plans which we needed to have in place. What to do if this happened and what to do if that happened, so many scenarios to consider to keep me safe all with an escape/bail out strategy.

A date was arranged when I could pick up my personal items. The counsellor had already phoned the police advising them of the proceedings, then she phoned them again once we had set the time. This was to ensure I had ready emergency support if He showed up; I only had to dial 000 and they would be there asap.

The day arrived. I had a window between 9.30am to 11.30am that He had set for me to collect my items. Simone came with me in my car and James was already there repairing the damage He had done to the ride-on mower. We said our hellos and then I went to work packing a few items into boxes. I started by going into one room at a time, checking the rooms to see if there were personal items of mine which were essential for me to have, or if He had taken items that I really wanted. As I packed each box, Simone took them and loaded the car. I focused on getting items together and getting out as quickly as possible. Also, I didn't want Simone or James to see me rattled.

After a while I became frantic. I felt I was taking too long; I did not want Him to turn up suddenly. I was scared, fearful, frightened of confrontation. I looked at my watch and thought it was 11.00am. Panic set in. I could feel an anxiety attack coming on. My breathing became irregular, I felt dizzy, light headed I could not remain still, I had to rush rush rush. James and Simone could see I was anxious and not coping. They got me to sit on a stool to have a glass or two of water, trying to settle me. I was grateful for this break in my frantic race to get everything done and get out.

Once I realized that it was only 10am not 11am, my breathing slowed and I relaxed a little. I had enough time to drink the two glasses of water before continuing.

I quickly packed a few other items before heading off. We could not get anything else into the car, and I needed to get out of there and away, back to safety. Both James and Simone were adamant that I was not to drive so Simone drove us back to her place where I was staying. Time to sit and sense some calmness move over me.

Back at the safehouse, as I called Simone's place. Over the coming weeks I kept my mind occupied playing word puzzles I had downloaded onto my notebook. I would challenge myself to get them completed as quickly as possible before I advanced to the next level. It was a great distraction from all the tensions.

Simone's family would soon be going on holidays for the year, but they were all still there with me. The grandchildren would come down in the evening before bed time and I would download a new word game for us all to play. We'd all lie on the fold-out couch (my bed), and go through the games on my notebook. I thoroughly enjoyed those times spent with the grandchildren. My children and grandchildren have always meant everything to me. Time spent with them was the most precious gift of all.

When I first moved in at Simone's, she gave me a beautiful packet of cards, self-care cards along with a lovely journalling notebook. I would take a new card out each day and along with the date I would write the saying down from the card. It was like my affirmation for the day. A new day a new page for a new affirmation. Underneath the affirmation I would then list all the things that I would like to achieve for that day, even if it was going down the street to the bank, or for groceries, or for a walk along the foreshore, and how far I would like to walk. Remember, to you it might seem nothing, to me I had been kept in total isolation for the last three years when neither of us was working, and for me everything was a huge feat. At the end of the day, I would tick the little box beside each task that I had completed. Although only small things, it felt like I had made some real achievements. Anything I did not manage to do; I would place a line through the little box and carry it over to the next page for the new day. I also had a little gratitude book where I could list three items that I was grateful for each day.

Some days it was a struggle to find three things but that would depend on what sort of day I had had. Usually when there were any communications with solicitors or real estate agents it was difficult. Most days I had four or five things I was grateful for; the tiniest moments are often the most precious.

So, you see, venturing out alone in the initial stages was a huge step for me.

While at Simone's my confidence grew more and more, and I ventured further afield. I went down to the boathouse to have a coffee and sit alone at the foreshore. I was nervous but I did it, this was a huge feat for me and I felt so good once I had achieved this. After a while, I would go down to the esplanade at least once a week to buy some fish and potato scallops (or potato cakes, depending on what state you come from). I loved my fish and chips; it was always such a treat. The first few times, I would take them back to eat them in the car, to hold the feeling of being safe. It took a while but I did eventually gain enough confidence to sit at one of the many tables on the foreshore and eat my fish. It was so nice feeling and smelling the fresh sea air saying hi to the people walking by.

Unfortunately, I could never venture far from the car as He still had the other set of car keys. To have the locks changed would run into the thousands of dollars, which I did not have (solicitors bills were running up). Instead, I purchased a steering lock. This gave me significant peace of mind and a feeling of security.

I was safe and I was growing in confidence, I felt like a kid in a lolly shop as over these past few months I had discovered there was so much to life out there for me to explore. Scary but fun. I had an open mind and was ready to learn and explore; it seemed so exciting. But the pressures and trauma triggers kept coming. I had to remain strong and keep learning as I continued my quest out of DV. There was still quite a journey to go yet.

Let's remind ourselves of some facts, thanks to the Australian Institute of Strangulation Prevention.4

Fifty-six percent of incidents happen during separation, actual or pending (remember, there is a person behind each of these statistics).

According to Red Rose Foundation webinar of Mar 2019, these are the predominant risk factors:
- Separation (actual or pending)
- Coercive control
- Stalking
- Intimate partner sexual violence
- Escalating violence including threats to kill
- Threats of suicide

Men who strangle their partners are among the most dangerous abusers out there
- Some strangle to kill
- Some strangle to show they can kill
- The act of strangulation symbolises an abuser's power and control over the victim
- Most victims of strangulation are women

A single act of strangulation can instil such fear that a victim can become trapped in a pattern of deadly control.[5]

RRF explains that non-lethal strangulation is one of the most significant red flags to homicide as well as premature death from strokes and other health issues.

As most victims of strangulation have no visible injuries or their injuries are too minor to photograph, opportunities for higher level criminal prosecution are often missed.[6]

Training is essential for police, ambulance, prosecutors, health services, DV and sexual assault services, and community service groups, to understand and develop heightened responses to non-lethal strangulation.[1]

Then we come to coercive control.

Coercive control is where offenders use patterns of abusive behaviours over time in a way that creates fear and denies the victim of freedom and independence. People, usually narcissists, who use coercive control may use physical or non-physical abusive behaviours, or a combination of both. The offenders constantly put an individual down, shaming, and humiliating them, making them doubt themselves or their abilities. Generally, they constantly use tactics that pressure or punish the other person.

Research from various sources identifies several triggers. Some common examples of coercive behaviour are:
- Isolating you from friends and family.
- Taking control over aspects of your everyday life, such as where you can go, who you can see, and what you can wear.
- Controlling everyday needs, such as finances, medication, food, or exercise.
- Monitoring or tracking everything you do.

- Depriving you access to support services, such as medical services.
- Repeatedly putting you down, such as saying you're worthless.
- Humiliating, degrading, or dehumanising you.
- Making threats or intimidating you.[7]

However, it is important to note that not everyone knows they are experiencing coercive control. For some it's not until we are out of the environment that we come to realise the signs. The penny drops so to speak.

With the support of RRF I went through the court system. This was traumatic within itself. As I fronted up to the court-house, I saw Him walking across the other side of the road. I panicked. Fear took over.

My counsellor had already arranged for me to wait for our hearing in a safe room. Although this room was secure, I could not control my panic as I sat there. Each time the door handle moved or the door opened, I got such a fright that it felt like you could have peeled me off the ceiling. My counsellor could see how fearful I was. She held my arm, trying to calm me. Although this was a little reassuring, it didn't stop my reactions. I was jumping out of my skin.

When we entered the courtroom, a police officer sat beside me, and my counsellor sat behind me. Once I saw Him in the same room, I started to shake uncontrollably. It was a horrific feeling. I couldn't wait to get out of the court-room.

The magistrate set a date for the hearing in a few weeks' time. I was devastated. I wanted it to be all over and done with.

Over the next few weeks, I went through my notes again, and forwarded them to my solicitor to review. My solicitor, although understanding, emphasised that it was a hard road to travel. I took some time to contemplate all this. The emotions I was going through did not help me at all. I felt like I was falling apart, I needed to get some control. So it was after much deliberation, I made the decision not to proceed. I could not sit in a courtroom with Him there on the other side.

I wrote a letter to the magistrate and drove to the courthouse to submit my letter of withdrawal.

> *At this stage I currently live with my daughter, who will be away travelling, until the end of this calendar year.*
>
> *After much deliberation and following text messages from my husband resulting in anxiety attacks, and inability to breath. Reliving the trauma from not only the past 40years but also the last few months leading up to my escaping from the perpetrator, in addition to ongoing text/emails from him since that date; for my own wellbeing I have decided at this stage to withdraw my application.*
>
> *I will have to leave it in the hands of God to keep me safe.*

I did not trust the legal system. A ruling does not stop a perpetrator.

As I stood at the courthouse counter, I was not conscious that I was crying; however, the tears were streaming down my face. They said they could not accept the letter, as it placed me at further risk. The tears kept flowing, it was like the floodgates had been opened. I was trying to hold it all together, but the tears kept coming. After a while, following some discussion with a few people in the courthouse, they gave me a form to complete, they still wouldn't take my letter.

I completed the form and one of the legal team witnessed it, making it clear to me that the magistrate would phone me to discuss the matter. At this stage, I didn't care. I wanted to finish this process, to close it, and get out of there. I left the courthouse and drove back to Simone's to relax and sleep. The day's events had totally drained me.

It took a few weeks to regain my strength.

I needed to move forward, but at my own pace. I needed to make the most of each moment of growing, of continuing with my life.

CHAPTER THREE

THE TRANSITION

I have long since learned, in life a girl hurts and sometimes cries, but you cannot see the depression in her eyes that she acquired in life because she just smiles. The pain is disguised behind a smiling face. - Anonymous

Years previously I had taken two different jobs in Victoria, one in the western side of the state, and then following this, one on the eastern side of the state in the Gippsland region. We had been away from the family for seven years; I was missing them. The decision was made, much as He resisted, that I finish my work in Victoria, and we would pack up and move back home.

Back in Queensland neither of us worked, although this did not stop Him from pressuring me to get a job. I spent my time restoring the garden so that it was presentable again, getting the veggie patch and herb garden back into shape, plus I was making large bamboo chimes. We had been back three years; they were tense times. He had control over all aspects of my everyday life, where I could go who I could see and He repeatedly put me down, humiliating and degrading me. I could not do anything right, there was constant criticism of everything I did. I felt like I was no more than a piece of dog shit on the ground, not worth even stomping on.

It was not long after this that I moved out (escaped) and was living at Simone's; meanwhile the house we had owned was placed on the market. We had discussed selling the property for over a year by then, and in that time, I had washed and repainted the entire interior of the house. We had bought new drapes for all the rooms and a new flat pack kitchen was installed, which helped to make the house more appealing. The house was beautiful, ready for sale at any time. The gardens I kept well weeded, and the veggie patch with all the herbs and companion plants were thriving; it looked inviting.

Once the house was on the market, He did not allow me back until after it was sold. He had decided that until He had moved everything, He wanted out of the house I could not re-enter. He would leave me only what He could not take. I had informed my solicitor of some of the items I would like; the list was small, half a page no large item. I could not move any heavy items on my own anyway. Although the list with my requested items was forwarded via solicitors, He disregarded it.

Throughout the process of selling the house, a lot of manipulation and game playing went on. I had to find the inner strength to stand firm, not get persuaded, stick to my principles. My counsellor was tremendous support. In the end your principles, your thoughts, your life cannot be nor should not be manipulated.

He was consistent and persistent in reminding me each fortnight when it was my turn to pay for the mortgage. We were taking it in turns to pay the mortgage. The payments were only a very small amount, but it was control again even in the subtlest of ways. Seven months earlier He had been consistently criticising and scolding me, insisting that I cash in my superannuation, constantly berating me with a barrage of criticism and put downs, yelling at me and never letting up on telling me how useless I was.

I was made to feel that everything was lost that I was not a person, I wasn't even worth pissing on. I felt I wasn't of any value to anyone or anything. Why was I still breathing? It was relentless. After a while you have near to no feelings, you exist. I don't know how or why I kept going. I had ignored his persistent requests to cash in my super, but worn down I conceded. He stood over me as I completed all the superannuation forms and spoke on the phone with the person from my superannuation fund. He kept telling me what I had to say to them, word for word, and yelled at me if I got it wrong.

I had hung onto the superannuation I'd accumulated in the past as it was like a security blanket for me, something I could fall back on. Taking it away left me with nothing to fall back on. I lost all sense of security; there was no fall back for me to live off. Nothing. And if the barrage of verbal abuse halted for a moment there was still the physical abuse. I felt desolate, isolated, bleak, and abandoned. But there was something inside me that stopped me from suicide; I don't know what it was. Perhaps you can call it an inner will to live to survive despite all adversity.

Over the years I had become an empty shell, I felt numb to everything, I was a robot that went through the motions of each day. Get up, go to work, go home, cook, wash, clean, then start the next day the same tasks repeated. I dared not venture into any shops on my way home for fear of the repercussions.

After all the children had left home before our trip down to Victoria so I could start working over in the Wimmera region He was summonsed to appear before the crime and misconduct commissioner to answer charges brought against him for threatening and attempting to injure a fellow work colleague. He had a violent temper, he kept it well camouflaged and under control while at work, well, the majority of the time. He would only bring it out at home, where no one else was around. On this one occasion, the facade had slipped, resulting in the accusations of attempting to inflict serious harm upon a work colleague. If it had not been for the tenacity and fortitude of our lawyer, charges could potentially have been laid against Him in the courts, the next step up so to speak. A settlement was made.

I felt like the entire episode swept right over me. I was so numb to any and every feeling. Events going on around me didn't hit home. Yes, there was concern, but I was so isolated and desolate that all I could do was run on autopilot as I went from day to day.

While at Simone's, with communication still ongoing with Him, there was a lot of arguing over small items. He wanted the thumb drive out of my car but He had removed this when the car went in for a service a few months prior. Goodness knows where he put it. Walking poles, he had the wrong ones; I apparently had his. So, Simone had to drop them off at James's place so He could pick up the correct ones and He would leave mine to be collected. Little items seemed to be any excuse to have an argument. When it came to our grandson's birthday, I had already purchased a present and sent it.

He wanted to know what I got; 'Send me a photo.' He said he would purchase and send a card for our grandsons on behalf of both of us.

Then he wanted my car. His younger brother was flying down from Far North Queensland and He wanted my car to drive his brother around. He had a perfectly good vehicle, but I was aware that his younger brother was interested in buying my car. This was mine. His demands were: - 'I've been stuck with the Ute, and want you to at least think about giving me a break from that.' As I was going to be away during the time He had requested the car, I let him know it was unavailable. He then changed the dates of when he wanted my car. Something was up? He stated I should not be concerned about there being anything underhanded; that the vehicle would not be damaged and would be returned clean and refueled, that He merely wanted a break from driving his vehicle. My response: 'I prefer to have my car as it is less pain for me driving with the bursitis.' Topic dropped.

I realized I had become stronger, I no longer had to comply with his demands. This was a new feeling. I felt I was gaining some of my dignity back.

Further skepticism related to the recent sale of the caravan where He had assured James (who purchased the caravan) that the monies would be split evenly and I would get half of the proceeds. Really? I knew I would never see any proceeds from the sale, and I never have to this day. I was prepared for that as I knew his only interests were monetary and in getting whatever he could for himself.

There are numerous times when He would text or email, applying pressure, asking me if this was really what I wanted. In the end, I had to ask my solicitor to send a letter of demand that He not contact me. Which He ignored. When Simone saw that He had sent a few emails within two days, hounding me, she replied on my behalf. Advising Him that it was too much to bombard me with numerous emails, and requesting He only send one email a day, advising Him I was going away for a while and I'd read His emails when I returned.

Not long after this I had to block his phone calls. My solicitor had stated to him that all communication was to be through our respective legal representatives.

When it came time for moving all our furniture after the sale of the property, He advised me He had signed the contract, and demanding I provide Him with sufficient funds so he could move out or He would leave all the moving costs to me. We were both on unemployment benefits at the time yet he still expected me to pay even when he had all the money from the sale of the caravan. Eventually, when he had moved out with everything he wanted, I did pay for the cleaners and the contractors to move all the other items, to get it all over and done with. He had not left much and most of these items I couldn't take. I was glad I went through one large box he had placed as rubbish to be thrown out. It was in the double garage. In the box was my mother's photo album along with other items I held dear and wanted to give to the children.

I had to purchase a new laptop as He insisted, He have the original one back, even though it was mine. He even used my email address as his, so I created a new one on my new laptop. I bought a new phone. He insisted on knowing what type of mobile I had purchased, and He then went and bought the same mobile phone. With my new laptop and new email address I contacted all my relatives and friends that I had not been allowed to communicate with over the years. It was nice not to have his oversight or commentary on everything I wrote.

I kept my days busy as I went through the process of the separation, adjusting, and managing the torments that He would visit upon me. It did not take Him long to manipulate our children with his lies. I remember vividly how I had gone around to James's to briefly talk about the incident of the strangulation. Some of the comments James made during our conversation, left me with no doubt of His manipulations. James would not have known some of the details of that day, as James had not been in the room where it happened until much later. He was filling James's head with lies. I decided not to try to clarify things with James as I could see it was traumatic enough for him to have to recall the incident of the strangulation. I asked James if he had sought counselling to help him through; he had not. It was not something he seemed to want or was prepared to do. I hope he does seek some help at a later stage.

This reinforced my resolve to keep the children out of any discussions, actions or contact with solicitors. I explained to all my children that I did not intend to go through all the details with them, I did not want them caught between their father and I. Our children each had their own respective families now and they were all old enough to make up their own minds. They were not aware of what had taken place over the years; this was more for their protection than anything else. I was not going to go through anything or sway them in any direction, as in the end the actual truth will and does come out.

It was after I was out of the marriage that my friends started to come out and say they had suspected He was a narcissist but they had not said anything to me of their suspicions. Over the years, they had repeatedly asked me how I was, as if they suspected something was not quite right. But rather than admit anything to them, with my feelings of shame, I would blindly cover it up.

Interesting fact...

Narcissistic Personality Disorder (NPD) causes problems in many areas of life and in close relationships. The following are some of the interpersonal issues that are often driven by symptoms of NPD:

- Overreacts
- Cannot take criticism
- Makes excuses for own flaws or failings
- Refuses to take responsibility
- Attempts to sway or manipulate others
- Hypercompetitive
- Only associates with people deemed to be on "their level"
- Reacts with rage
- Shames others
- Emotionally neglectful
- Does not listen
- Interrupts often [8]

He was a person who would have no qualms in emotionally hurting even his own children.

Many years prior when we were living in Far North Queensland, we were cleaning out the tray of the bird cage which was holding Simone's two love birds. She had a yellow and a blue love bird. The two younger boys had accidentally opened the cage and let the birds out. We were devastated; how were we going to get them back. We tried a few tactics, but nothing worked. Her father said to Simone, it is okay we will get a rifle and shoot them down. I went to the pet store and brought two blue love birds for her, not the same I know, but I could not see her so upset.

This man had advised Simone's husband that if he wanted to give flowers to Simone at any time, to go to the cemetery and collect the flowers from the grave sites. I am not joking. He actually said this. Who does that? This was his daughter!!!

In the last three years I was with Him, whenever I went out it had to be with his approval and in his company. Twice a year I was allowed to go shopping with my daughter, or sometimes Annie. I really looked forward to our shopping days. I would save up and loved to buy shoes and clothes. Don't most women?

I would arrive at Simone's early in the morning (she lived an hour away on the east coast of Brisbane). We would spend much of the day browsing the shops, having cups of coffee, morning and afternoon teas, then more shopping. It was the best of times. Come time to head home and I would dread it. Once home as soon as I walked through the door, I was grilled about what I had spent. He already knew, as he had already checked online to see the bank transactions. I had to explain every one of them and show him the items I had purchased. There was always some sarcastic comment: 'You're going to look fat in that,' or 'That looks awful,' 'What made you get that?' 'Where are you going to wear that?' and so on.

I got used to not saying anything or talking, as everything was twisted around. He consistently made me feel I was a dumb arse. I was out of energy, fearful and dejected, and resigned myself to the fact that nothing would change. He made me believe I was not worth anything at all. Hear it enough times and you believe it. As far as He was concerned, I should be out there getting a job and bringing the money in. He was used to buying whatever He wanted. Since returning to Queensland from Victoria, my refusal to work was cramping his style and He was pressuring me to get that job. He would list the jobs I could apply for; He would always type up a covering letter for my application. I continued to stay silent, remaining steadfast in my resolve. It was my conscious decision not to work again, not yet anyway, you might say this was my first attempts at resistance, (and I paid for it as the abuse amplified). I had worked these past eleven years while He stayed home doing whatever, I never knew. As I saw it, it was his turn to work.

While I was at Simone's, I needed to keep myself organised. And preparing for the future regarding care for the kids in the event I should die was another task I needed to attend to. I booked an appointment with the public trustee. I had made notes over the past few months of what I wanted done if I died, speaking with my doctor on occasion regarding my statement of choices. This is a very important document to complete as you can outline what you do and do not want to happen when you are dying which is then registered with the state. I completed it first with my doctor, as the appointment with the public trustee was quite a few weeks off. This gave me time to really think about what I wanted, how property and assets should be divided among the children. I had it more or less sorted in my thoughts but when I made the appointment, they sent through a list of items that I should consider prior to the meeting in order to be efficient and complete everything on the day. This was very useful as I was able to write it all down, going over it time and again to ensure that this was exactly what I wanted.

The day for the meeting with the public trustee arrived and I had a very productive meeting. There were a few things I needed to be made aware of, for example the enduring power of attorney, when it comes into effect, and how to ensure it is only initiated in certain circumstances under rigid guidelines. When it came to the choices and decisions I had made as regards the disbursement of property and assets, as I had not divided these equally, it was explained that it was important to be aware of the potential for my wishes to be contested upon my death, and therefore I need to know what documents to complete so that if my will was contested my wishes could not be changed. It was not that I had a lot in terms of assets, but what I did have I wanted to make sure it went where I wanted, not what someone else thought.

Completing these tasks was a great distraction for me, allowing me to focus on something else beyond feeling sorry for myself, or reliving the trauma in my mind. I was practicing and trying so hard not to go into a spiral of negative thoughts and instead remain positive, forever the optimist.

It was not until the property was sold that the ongoing discussions began between our solicitors for the split in assets. He wanted more than his fair share; I wanted out. Finally, there was some agreement, with me conceding to a lot less than half, to be out and rid of Him. The solicitors had submitted the documents to the family law courts. Now it was a matter of waiting. Patience is not my best attribute; however, this journey has made me realise that I need to learn and experience more about patience, that I needed to slow down.

So, another task I was to set for myself was that, learning patience. A lot of it came down to thought patterns and breathing. I learnt about this through the books that came to me. I resigned myself to letting it be - everything will happen in its own good time. It would just be nice if it happened yesterday. But then I would miss out on the journey and the learnings I needed.

It was now Spring. Surprisingly the family court (under the Family Law Act 1975 in the Federal Circuit and Family Court of Australia (Division 2)) approved the terms of settlement in only a few weeks. I was not only surprised when my solicitor contacted me to advise me of this, but also relieved to be finally rid of Him. He no longer had any financial hold over me.

Over the next week, even though He had emptied out the bank accounts we had, they still had to be closed. I knew he would not bother, so I visited each bank and closed all the accounts. It was a week or two later that He finally posted my car keys as per the court agreement. SAFE AT LAST. Although, now that I was in the habit of placing the steering lock on the car, I felt it was a good habit to continue.

Simone and family had taken off for their holiday around Australia at the start of winter, so I was renting the downstairs area plus looking after the dog and sharing the house with another woman, Chrystal, who had also come out of a violent relationship. She had young children, who were lovely. It did not take us long to fit in and get along. The kids were terrific. The younger one would come downstairs after kindy and take a running dive onto my lap as I sat in front of the TV. She would have her cuddle and then sit with me to watch the TV as I talked her through whatever events or shows we were watching. She was a very smart child, but slow to communicate effectively; this would improve with time. The older daughter loved to live in what she called her 'beach house by the sea.' She was also infatuated with the dog, an American Staffy, a huge dog. She was only a fraction taller than him. Coming home from school, she would look for him. We used to be amazed at how much control such a little girl could have over such an enormous dog. When told to sit he would sit. Anytime she had given him a command, he would follow obediently.

Chrystal and I got into a routine, once the girls were in bed at night. We would both sit down and talk through the day's events, hers with her ex and I with mine. We would talk for hours, helping each other as we discussed the different ways of getting through each battle or challenge that came our way. We talked of our previous lives growing up, family and friends. We formed a special bond, which I treasured and still do to this day.

While living there, Chrystal met a man who was so caring, they were a perfect match. It was lovely to see. I was really happy for them.

It was Chrystal who sent me the caption 'Spot the girl who stays in motion' more on this in chapter four.

CHAPTER FOUR

SUPPORT

Innocent girls speak only truth, and from the heart.

It is so helpful and enlightening when you talk about what you are going through with your counsellor. They put everything into perspective. Something I learnt in my working career, during a course on risk management, was that it is more effective to work on a problem or situation than it is to working while in it. I suppose it is a bit like the 'You cannot see the forest for the trees' saying. You are too close to the problem and need to step away, to distance yourself from the issues so you can work out how or what you can do to address the problem or issue. Although this was related to work, I also found it useful in everyday life. As I was living in trauma day to day and not slowing down, not seeing the forest. But when you leave due to a DV situation, initially it is so difficult to think with clarity, and for me it was also learning to slow down. I found my mind was racing in all different directions with various scenarios. This is where the counsellors are so helpful, listening and putting events into perspective.

One counsellor had explained to me that what I had been through was not an occasional traumatic event but what I had been experiencing was akin to walking on eggshells 24/7 for 40 years, and this had to have had some effect.[1]

It was early in the separation that I asked my doctor to provide me with a referral to a psychologist. I needed to make sure I was not being impractical and to have help in providing me with strategies, I needed help with tactics to cope with the all the emotions I was experiencing. One useful piece of advice I received was to stop and breathe whenever I became anxious. My psychologist diagnosed PTSD. I had what I called brownouts, I would be talking about a situation and when I was beginning to feel stressed, an incident of DV, I would go completely blank. It would take me a few moments before I returned to the conversation and had to be reminded what the conversation was about. I became used to asking about the subject we were discussing, so I could pick up and continue. Breathing would help me through.

On my follow-up visit I informed my psychologist of the task I'd set myself of writing affirmations and listing all the things I wanted to achieve for each day and recording all the things I was grateful for. My psychologist commented that I was very organised and heading in the right direction, and to keep up the great work.

I know I received great support from my counsellors and they were there whenever I needed them, or very soon after on the phone. Initially I found it hard to talk about my feelings as for years I had kept my emotions so close; I buried them, never to be spoken about. Once I started talking, it began to pour out. I think this was down to building a good rapport and trust with my counsellor. I had bottled up and hidden my feelings for so many years in my case over forty years so there was quite a bit to come out.

What is the meaning of trauma: 9
- an injury (such as a wound) to living tissue caused by an extrinsic agent
- a disordered psychic or behavioural state resulting from severe mental or emotional stress or physical injury
- an emotional upset

Emotions, the feelings, take over; they are hard to control. But it is interesting to look at the meaning and/or synonyms of the word.
- a conscious mental reaction (such as anger or fear) subjectively experienced as a strong feeling usually directed toward a specific object and typically accompanied by physiological and behavioural changes in the body
- a state of feeling
- the affective aspect of consciousness – feeling

There has been research conducted which identifies the following as distinct emotions we all have: Interest, Joy, Surprise, Sadness, Anger, Disgust, Contempt, Self-Hostility, Fear, Shame, Shyness, and Guilt. 17

When bottled-up, these emotions, hide within your body, within your muscles, thereby affect your entire physical body. Breathing correctly is immensely important (as I was reminded by a friend and my psychologist) and is crucial to our wellbeing. I recall my first major anxiety attack due to trauma.

Although the police officer at the time I made the report advised me that He had admitted to the non-lethal strangulation, now in a letter from his solicitor, he was denying that He was the perpetrator and said that it was my fault that he threw me to the floor and strangled me.

This took my breath away. I was in shock and shaken, literally unable to breathe. Fortunately, Simone was there, and she hugged me so tight, yelling into my ear, 'Breathe Mum, just breathe.' She kept saying this over and over.

Simone is very strong, so it was a solid hug, it made me feel safe. It took some time for me to work through the anxiety, starting with small, deliberate breaths, and trying to keep the breathing to a slow yet steady pace, little by little taking deeper breaths till I regained my normal breathing pattern.

*

There was one day of the week I really looked forward to: Sundays. I had begun to volunteer at one of the local opportunity shops, where I had hit it off instantly with a few of the other girls volunteering, especially Kate. Kate actually changed one of her volunteering week days to a Sunday so we could work together. I felt so humbled by this, and we had so much fun, Kate was a great support to me.

People do come into your life for a reason, it is not only the books that come to you. Kate taught me so much about narcissists (her mother was one). We had a small book section at the opportunity shop and Kate, who had gone through a different type of trauma relating to her working life, enjoyed sorting through the books. As she came across one that she felt might help me or I might be interested in, she would put it aside for me to purchase at the end of the day. The girls I worked with were wonderful, we all supported each other which was magical. We would have so much fun talking with clients, helping others out, it always left me with a great feeling at the end of the day. There is nothing like the feeling of contributing and helping someone out. The different conversations we had with clients were lifegiving. It was a lovely feeling talking about places lived and travelled in Australia, helping them to find what they were looking for in the store. It was all so good.

Volunteering at the opportunity shop, reading my books and journalling, having chats with people, most times total strangers, I really started to enjoy the contact with people in the community, even if it was only for that one time. It was exhilarating and interesting.

I had joined the local library and inadvertently, between the books from the library and the books Kate would find for me I was taken on the most amazing journey of learning and adventure. There is a saying that a book comes to you for a reason. Well, mine certainly did, and what is more they flowed on from one other.

I started with a new type of journalling. I would write down the title of the book and author, then whenever a sentence or paragraph resonated with me, I would write it in my new journal along with the page number from the book. I cannot recommend journalling enough, especially to help you learn how to work through life and its traumas. I am still so totally amazed by the flow and progression of the books I have read and how they took me on such a wonderful learning experience.

I still had my counsellor phoning me once or twice a week, depending on how I was coping. We would talk through the events of the week, how I was progressing, what road blocks I had, if any, and how to progress forward. The journalling added to this, helping me so much. I had two journal books now; I was still writing down my affirmations for the day and listing what I wanted to accomplish for the day, along with completing my grateful diary each day. I had gone through two packets of cards. The other journal contained the quotes that resonated with me from the wonderful books I was reading.

I went down to the newsagents and novelty shops looking for more packets of inspirational cards or little books with affirmations. None appealed to me. I had learnt over time, to let my instincts guide me. After searching through various shops, I did eventually find the little books that I liked. They were lovely, and all quite different, so I bought three of them. Again, I copied the saying from each page, as the affirmation for the day, into my daily journal book. And after a while, here too it became evident that the little books flowed on from one another the same as the books from the library and opportunity shop did. This was fascinating to me; I felt something was guiding me.

There are many affirmations available to us, enjoy the search of finding little books or cards with affirmations to help you through on your journey. Some of these might not appeal, pass them by as you only require the affirmations that ring true for you and help you on your journey. Affirmations inspire you, enhance your confidence, give you belief and strength.

I have always had the philosophy not only throughout my working life but for life in general, that if you can make one person smile a day it has been a good day. That does not have to mean you need an in-depth conversation, but a smile as you walk by them in the street. They might look upset or glum, but if I can bring a smile to their face, it has been a great day.

I was so grateful for the support from my relatives overseas, the encouragement they gave me about how I could get through this and come out stronger, more self-assured. I was very fortunate we had made contact again. Everyone was supportive, it was enormously encouraging for me.

I emailed an old school friend, Totty, to inform him of the separation, not too many details, that I was out and safe and needed Totty to be aware that He was using my old email address, and if Totty needed to contact me what my new email address was. I wanted to touch base with my girlfriend Renee as I no longer had her contact details - they were on the old laptop, which He had. She had been through a break up herself some years previously. She was someone I was comfortable talking to. Fortunately, after some time Totty passed on Renee's email address and phone number.

Friends come and go but a best friend will always find their way back to your heart. Making contact with my old school friends Renee turned out to be one of the best supports I have had.

At first, I started to tell Renee little by little about what I had been through with the domestic violence. It was good to talk it out with someone besides my counsellor, to have someone else to bounce off. Renee herself had not had a good experience with the man she was with for over twenty years. It was not due to domestic violence but she had been left heartbroken. Some men can be so cruel.

It helped me to tell her some of my life events with Him, as she had also known Him in our school years. It was during this time that I spoke with Renee about my little books and using them as affirmations for the day. I also told her what the psychologist had said regarding what I was doing with these affirmations and the gratitude books, and how it was setting me on my path to recovery. It was a matter of time now. Renee liked the idea, so I commenced the daily routine of sending a text with the affirmation for the day and she would reply, commenting on the saying/affirmation.

Renee started to enjoy these and as it appeared to help us both, it became a thing for us to look forward to. So I continued on, each morning sending Renee a text with the saying for the day. After some time, I was no longer sure if she enjoyed them or not, so I offered to stop sending them. But she made it clear that she liked receiving her daily texts. I would like to feel it helped us both, it was our unspoken way of keeping tabs on each other to make sure we were ok. I purchased a few of these little books and posted them to her so she could enjoy having her own. We were to continue this for over a year till we both progressed and realised it was time to move on, it would be ok. For me, I still write up my affirmation for the day along with the objectives I'd like to achieve, I don't feel I'm ready to stop yet. Besides, I enjoy writing up the new one for the day and seeing what comes my way.

During this time at Simone's place, Renee and I would occasionally catch up with a phone call. The phone calls went for hours. When Renee and I were at high school, we sometimes stayed at each other's place on the weekends. I vividly remember we would talk nearly most of the night, until we fell asleep with exhaustion. Nothing had changed.

*

Out of dark places come great support and learnings.

The Rabbit Hole – A Very Dark Place

A few months after I had escaped, and I was struggling to understand so many experiences and feelings I was going through. I would have phone calls with Red. Red was a quiet type, not ever giving too much away, whereas I found it very easy to talk to him. I felt I became a regular chatterbox whenever we spoke on the phone.

Red had a family member who had an awful experience and Red was struggling to understand the abuse and trauma she suffered, needing to see it from her point of view perhaps - I was not quite sure. There was one occasion I was on the phone with Red, when I found myself going down what I call the rabbit hole.

I was trying to explain the emotions that I went through, trying to explain the circumstances of the domestic violence I had experienced. I went through the events that happened to me, describing them to Red - only the strangulation - a very brief overview. I was happy to help Red gain some understanding of what it might have been like for his family member. Although not the same as mine, her experiences had also been traumatic. I hoped I was helping him anyway.

Some questions tested me, but if I could help him understand a little, I felt it was worthwhile.

But on this occasion, unfortunately, I was taken to a place I had not expected to go. It happened so quickly. I went down the rabbit hole. It was a very dark place. I had never had an experience like this before. I was reliving all the shame and disgust I felt towards myself and this feeling of worthlessness, it just came out of my mouth and I could not stop it.

I had to end the phone call, I was out of control, feelings of worthlessness kept me spiraling down and down.

I could not seem to get out of this dark place, I cried uncontrollably. It is hard to explain this feeling of complete and absolute despair, of not being able to talk to anyone over the years of the violence, and of how desolate I felt.

Visiting a dark place is something I believe we all must experience at some point, to be able to move forward. If I had not gone down the rabbit hole, I do not feel I would have moved forward in my journey so quickly. My deep regret, though, is my sense that Red felt responsible in some way for my going down the rabbit hole. He was not to know he was just trying to understand. It just happened out of the blue.

But I needed to take the rabbit's journey, to be able to feel the emotions the domestic violence had caused, to experience the thoughts and feelings, and be with them, processing them.

This loss, this disconnection, is at the root of all our feelings of fear, of not being good enough, of feeling unworthy. Finding myself in the dark - the not knowing yet learning to get really comfy with it. I was meeting parts of myself I didn't like. I was being totally open and, in the process, I started to shed what no longer served me. I learnt not to hold back, push down or suppress anything but to feel and express it all.

I'd been told over and over, in a million different ways, that I was unworthy, unfit, and that I had no value. I needed to tear this crap down and start to trust myself, my inner self.

I later learnt that in life you don't go back to the past to see if it still hurts, the pain of yesterday motivations the strength of today. 12

Do we all experience this dark place? I cannot speak for others but through my learnings it appears we do.

I discussed this phone call and the rabbit hole with my counsellor a few days later, as I was such a mess. She suggested I start to write these feelings up in a journal, like I was doing with the books I had read. She explained that going down the rabbit hole had proved a few things:

1. Although I love to help people, I was not ready yet.
2. When events happened that took me down near the rabbit hole I needed to take the next day off, go for a walk, read, paint my nails, do something that was a distraction.
3. There were a few events that had occurred one after another in just a few days and this had brought me grief, this being the third was, **'Too Much.'**

On reflection she was right.[1]

It is really hard when we are faced with not just difficulties but also challenges. They just seem to be too hard to handle. But we can and do manage to struggle our way through. This is where we grow and find purpose to our lives.

After the property and assets were approved by the courts, I applied for a job and was appointed to the position, a new one created for the region.

As Renee tried but could not make it to Queensland for a holiday, I had mentioned that I really needed a holiday, to get away and actually have a break. Something I had not ever done, or was allowed to do, despite Simone asking me to travel with her to Italy for a holiday twice, it was unfortunately not to be, I was not allowed. Now I could afford to travel down to visit, Renee and I set some dates in the new year.

Renee was there to greet me at the airport and over the next few weeks she drove me around all the old haunts. Places change so much. We drove past the home where I grew up, through the towns I used to travel through to go to school in Melbourne. There were many places and much to see, all the changes, but I still recognised some of the old landmarks and enjoyed seeing the beautiful countryside in Victoria's Dandenong's that I knew well growing up.

It was good to catch up face to face. Renee had arranged for a few more school friends to come and visit; it was daunting to say the least with the feelings I had to go through to maintain any sort of confidence. However, I had done this for years, covering up my true feelings of fear, portraying a happy relationship. Now that I was out, I decided to talk of some of the events, at least in a brief form. Finding my way was still scary.

Before I left for my holiday in Victoria, Renee had told me she had not been to the beach in years, so I asked my brother if we could stay in his holiday house on the southern coast for a few days. He graciously agreed. Renee and I later went on a road trip - well, a small one; it was just a drive down to my brother's holiday house on the coast.

Down at the holiday house my brother and Renee would go for long walks on the beach. It was good that they had each other's company and it was easy for them to get along. I sat on the rocks and enjoyed watching all the different birdlife, taking photos, and looking for shells close by. I still had a bung knee meaning I could not walk too far.

Our road trip, both down and back, was full of jokes and laughter. We stopped off at all the little coves and were amazed and appreciative of the magnificent scenery along the southern coast on our way back home. It was a thoroughly enjoyable time.

The entire holiday was like a journey back to my roots. I left to return home to Queensland feeling totally rejuvenated. I am grateful to Renee for her care, time, and support.

Little Bites

It was September of 2022; I wrote these notes at the time of one of my many phone support calls with my counsellor.

- Journey – manage your uncomfortable feelings, they are symbolic – defining an endpoint in the journey.
- I know that I can get to the other side.
- I had to manage awful situations - 'I am a survivor.'
- Be stronger and more determined. (It is within each of us.)
- I am not ready to take on other people's matters this soon.
- I am incredibly in tune with myself and the dark emotions, the down and dark times, are making me stronger.
- It does not feel good, but these emotions and feelings do serve a purpose.
- Keep a personal diary, even dot points on how to manage and tolerate the different circumstances that come my way. Events happen and I need to learn how to manage them.

Next day, digest the events, thoughts, emotions, feelings and take time out.

The constant throughout this support call was, 'Keep taking little steps, not big chunks.'

The very last comment about taking little steps I summarised as little bites is one I took to heart, finding it helpful. I had to keep reminding myself of this, as I was used to managing multiple tasks throughout my working career, dealing with crises, multiple issues at once, it was all go go go. Breaking it down and taking little bites is something that did not come easy to me when applying this to my personal life, to myself. With others, I had all the patience in the world; however, none for myself, as I was always challenging myself. I had to keep improving and to keep a lid on everything to protect the children, provide for them as best as I could.

I had to learn to break things down into smaller pieces, control myself and manage each issue one at a time, and I found this extremely difficult; however, over time and with concerted practice, once learnt it became easier. Although I still need to pull myself up now and then.

Traumas take place continually, more challenges, more learning, more hurdles to overcome, but it is true, you do become stronger after having moved through each one. The emphasis, for each one, is little bites, one at a time. The other part of this is to reflect, what is life telling me? Once I had escaped and was out, I found that whenever life was travelling along well, whenever I started to feel comfortable, an event would take place that triggered another challenging episode.

Trauma, the gift that keeps giving.

> *'Spot the girl who stays in motion*
> *She spins so fast so she won't fall*
> *She's built a wall with her achievements*
> *To keep out the question*
> *Without it, is she worth anything at all?'* ~ *Anonymous*

This is such an appropriate saying that describes just how I was feeling. It took me through many a battle as I tried to come to terms with myself and regain my self-worth.

We worry that we're seen as 'too much', while at the same time we struggle with the feeling that we are not enough. We're scared to come undone, because how will we ever put it all back together again? There will be a not knowing. I didn't know how I'd be judged or perceived, but standing within my own ability, my own strength and force, expressing myself and creating life on my own terms, knowing what I wanted, I found that trusting in myself was exactly what I needed to do. This takes tenacity.

My counsellor had advised me I was to learn to say 'No' and to put up boundaries, my boundaries. I had not done either of these things before. I had not put-up boundaries. It was suggested that I write down things that trigger a reaction in me then review this and ask why did they create this trigger. Unpack it (I used to hear Simone saying this to her clients).

Sitting with your feelings, your emotions, is not an easy thing to do. Feelings of suicide come over you, but then you ask yourself, for what purpose? To run away from a situation, not face up to the challenge? And why would I give Him the satisfaction? This was definitely not the answer. All these challenges that were coming my way could easily break me, but I dug my heals in; what does not break you makes you. I was going to maintain my resilience; I am a survivor.

Journalling does help, although I have never been one to journal my deep personal feelings, only the events that happen around me, or writings from the books I have read - not my inner most feelings. Sounds convoluted, doesn't it? Everyone is different though. On occasion I would diarise my deepest feelings, though: I kept it going for a few months recording how different events affected me and how they made me feel. It was incredibly useful. I recommend this to anyone. Although it is very difficult, and it did take me some time to record my feelings and thoughts it was good to have time out to write. I've always felt that when I write something down, I've released it from within myself, even if it is in an email to a friend. But a journal is better. It is immediate and I feel much better for it like a weight has been lifted and I no longer have to carry it. Similarly, you can look back and reflect.

It was a new experience to slow down and learn to sit with an emotion, to unpack it and then move forward from it. My support person stated on one occasion 'I'm amazed you managed this for so long. Lots of other people would give up.' That was a boost to the ego. She suggested I look on line and read about the window of tolerance; she sent a few links. This helped me to understand further the journey I needed to take. This provided some explanation of what I was experiencing.

It was another occasion with one of my phone support calls from my counsellor, when I was feeling like a yoyo, not sure of anything. They reiterated that this was my journey. I did not have to rush to get back into the workforce. I will know when it is time to return to work (besides, my solicitor had advised me to have a break). My support person recapped, I must live where I want and where I feel happy. My counsellor did say that I have this tendency to take things head on, and that this is not necessarily always the best of ways. Later I was to learn that this was true. I needed to remember to **take bite sizes, it is a journey, not a sprint.**

Challenges will continue to come your way; as they did for me. It is not only a test of how you cope with each challenge but how you work through each one. However, it does make you stronger.

I was putting the pressure on myself again; so used to years of rapid multitasking. I had thrived for years in jobs that pushed me to expand my ability and thinking, to consider numerous things at once, and I loved this, as it made me feel alive, I was making a difference to others people's lives, encouraging them, mentoring them. There is nothing more satisfying than seeing someone learn and grown. It also helped me to escape from thoughts of my homelife. But now I was finding it extremely difficult to slow down.

I was reminded of what Simone had said to me. 'Think where you'll be in two or five years time.'

The encouraging comments from my support person helped me gain confidence. She stated she had never heard defeat in my voice: 'You have inner wisdom in abundance,' 'You have an amazing amount of wisdom and purpose;' 'Your purpose is still evolving.' I was amazed by these comments as I did not feel wise or that I have this so-called wisdom and purpose. I was just little old me trying to cope and get through all the challenges and events coming at me; I was the one learning now. These comments were nevertheless a great boost to my confidence, confidence for me to keep moving forward in life no matter what the obstacles or where I was going.

Patience, I continued to find, was a test for me, and if I was to grow and evolve this would need to be overcome. Emotions were exhausting, they drained me of energy. Sometimes I needed to have an adrenaline reset. Feelings of dizziness would take me by surprise, which I learned was quite normal for a victim of domestic violence, and suffering from emotional exhaustion, would likely last for a while. *Every breath is moving forward.* While this was really helpful, and humbling it was also extremely exhausting.

As my support person explained I was to learn how to manage my trauma. I do not have to please other people especially if they are triggering the trauma. I needed to hold my trauma with the respect it deserved. Do not take others' emotions on. It became more evident that I had to look after myself only. Something that I had not done before and definitely did not come naturally. I felt that I was being selfish, might sound silly but that was my emotion around it. I needed to focus on restoring my concept of self, by doing the things I loved and lost sight of during the relationship, to try out brand-new hobbies. It's more about that notion of self-expansion, of introducing new perspectives and experiences into my life.

After talking with Renee, she mentioned that one of our school friends who was in a not-too-pleasant relationship and was still working through it had been exploring how to help herself, how to learn and grow in her own journey. It was on this journey that she completed a personality test online.

Anyone can do this, it is by Myers & Briggs [14], I was hesitantly surprised with my personality type.

I felt maybe this might help me to better understand my personal obstacles. Subsequently, I completed this on-line test. I found my results interesting, along with the fact my personality type is considered rare as it is estimated that only 1-2 per cent of the population have this personality type, due to a few unique combinations of traits such as being introverted, intuitive, and personal feelings, all together it is uncommon among most people. I was surprised; wasn't I like most people?

Apparently, I'm guided by a deeply considered set of personal values. Being intensely idealistic, and can clearly imagine a happier and more perfect future. I can become discouraged by the harsh realities of the present, but I'm typically motivated and persistent in taking positive action nonetheless, and I feel a fundamental drive to do what I can to make the world a better place. This correlated with what my counsellor had been saying to me.

It seems I 'want a meaningful life and deep connections with other people. I don't tend to share myself freely but appreciate emotional intimacy with a select, committed few' which is quite true. Although my 'rich inner life can sometimes make me seem mysterious or private to others, I profoundly value authentic connections with people I trust.' This came to fruition when the receptionist at my medical centre commented that she perceived me as very private person. I didn't think I was, as since my escape I had adopted a very cautious approach when it came to including people into my circle. But it did me good to hear it, an observation from another person. Made me reflect on this.

The report identified that I have 'a unique ability to intuit others' emotions and motivations, and will often know how someone else is feeling before that person knows it himself. I trust my insight about others and have strong faith in my ability to read people. Although I am sensitive, I'm also reserved; a private sort, and selective about sharing intimate thoughts and feelings.' I must agree, I can't refute this analogy.

*

With all my journalling, reading and texting/emails to and from friends, family and my counsellor, I felt the need to let them know how I was travelling. It was only the first step, I know, but I could never have progressed through these few months without their support.

It is amazing how people can be very supportive and rally around you when you yourself feel lost. I will be forever grateful for the support I received from friends old and new.

Later I sent a text to them all, with the following words:

'Hi, I'm sending this text message to you all individually as individually you have been there to support me, be it over a long or a short time. You are all very diverse yet for me the balance of your personalities and care is perfect. Be it email, text, phone, colleagues, or lunch, you have helped me to stay focused and on track (plus keep my head on so to speak). I can never express my gratitude to you. I am fortunate to have you as friends. Please know that I love and care for you all deeply. And I hope to catch up with you all over the next 12 months. I have changed the ending and my journey now begins. Enough of the soppy stuff, please know I am very grateful.'

CHAPTER FIVE

WET FISH MOMENTS

We can all achieve anything that we put our minds to, but it takes more. It takes facing our fears, perseverance and actions.

'You will be faced with many challenges along this journey.' These wise words from my counsellor rang true.

Be prepared, as you will. I found that although what I call "wet fish moments" were stressful, I remained positive in the belief that 'this too shall pass.' I knew that I would be able to work through and come out the other side, even though some events were challenging and really tested me.

Part of the survival journey once you are away from the abusive relationship is finding the right place to live. I was fortunate that my daughter took me in. She and her husband required an income for the property to cover the cost of rates and insurance etc and someone to look after their dog while they were travelling around Australia. My rent payments would not be enough though. As I indicated in chapter three, this is how I came to meet Chrystal and her two small children; like me, she was escaping from a domestic violence relationship, and was renting part of the house for herself and her children. We clicked straight away and really supported each other through our respective journeys.

With the property and asset settlement from the sale of the house and land approved by the courts, being in full-time employment meant I could look for a property to purchase for myself. However, in a market where prices were rising daily, it was difficult; a lot of my time was spent on the internet looking up places for sale then attending inspections on the weekends.

The extracts further in this chapter are copies of emails which will provide some idea relating to more wet fish moments, specifically pertaining to the incident of Simone's dog.

The emails are between Bubbles and me, as she helped me through these tough times. She listened, was non-judgemental and allowed me to write events out without criticism. These describe only a few challenges/wet fish moments that I sent to her explaining what I faced the few months after I had escaped.

Hi Bubbles

Thank you for the offer of a roof over my head, I cannot begin to tell you how much I appreciate it.

As regards buying the townhouse my thoughts were to rent some rooms out to cover the cost of the body corporate and rates etc. I've inspected more than a few and come to realise I'm not going to last too long with stairs, I haven't seen the specialist from the Hospital yet, and although the cortisone injection into my knee has helped immensely, at least I can walk (with a limp) I have minimal cartilage in my knee, same leg as the bursitis, stairs in a townhouse are painful it's not worth it. Plus, many properties are very expensive. I got really disheartened.

Finally found a listed place to look at, after missing a few turns and having to find my way again it was whilst I was walking along the drive following the signs for the inspection, I tripped and fell. Face planted on the bitumen, phone and bag went flying. After I picked myself up, I then proceeded to pick up phone etc, and stood up, blood pouring out of me as it always does from a head/face injury. I found a face mask to slow the bleeding. Ok, I've been given three warnings from the angels yet I didn't listen, I promptly turned around went back to the car, tried to clean myself up then drove home and sat in front of the TV for the rest of the day.

I've always tried to stay positive and focused, could be the weather, but I'm feeling flat last few days. Could also be Optus.

Well, isn't that a story.

I received an email from Optus on Sat they had been hacked and customers personal details had been stolen. Monday, I tootled off to the Queensland transport office to get a new Licence, couldn't get the computer screen to give me a ticket, then a young guy came along and lightly touched the screen and got one. Not a good start, but grateful to the young guy. Got talking to a few ladies whilst we were waiting, no point us all sitting there in silence and not talking. Anyway, up I go when my number was called. Show them the email from Optus, 'oh no you have to go to the police station and make a report, you also have to complete a Statutory Declaration.' Off I go to the police station. 'Oh no' I was told, 'you have to report it *on line to the cyber report website, you don't need a stat dec??!!!!'*

Nonetheless I came back and tried to report it via the cyber website, no luck figured I'd give it a miss and read a book, patience can be obtained through other distractions.

Next day I got up and tried the cyber website again. Success, I have a report number to show the police station person. Off I trot to the police station where the nice lady gave me a letter after I showed her the cyber number and gave her my licence. I asked fortunately, about the Stat Dec, 'oh yes you will have to complete one, we don't have anyone here at the moment, but you can get it signed by a JP at the stationery shop further down the road.' Off I drive down the road, the guy was very helpful. All signed, let's go, off to the Qld transport, ran into the lovely girl next door (another story further down) and had a chat with her, Lola is her name, she and her husband helped me two weeks ago. They have a one-year-old baby boy, lovely couple. She told me that Qld Transport had changed the process. Great.

I walked around the corner to the next block, and they were queuing out the door. Bloody terrific. I joined the queue, there was someone from the Qld transport explaining it all outside to the people lining up for a new licence. Apparently on Monday night Qld transport got the directive to issue all those affected with a new licence, didn't need to go through all the palaver that I'd been told to go through. As we were in the line, I got talking to a few people, as you do. The woman behind me had her identity stolen twice before in the last few years. This made it very real. Interestingly she used to work in the areas of the *banks where they monitor these issues and conduct risk assessments etc for the banks in such events as this and/or the Governments go to war. She then went on to tell me that if Australia went to war people with over a certain amount in their bank accounts, would lose the excess above that amount. Meaning that I would lose anything over this amount as it would go to fund the war efforts etc etc. Are you shitting me!!!*

Big message she kept putting across was do not put all your eggs in one basket. Good old saying and very true. Very kind of her to pass on such good intel. I had been restricted in knowing all our finances only told what He decided to let me know, now that I had control of my asset along with everything else, all information I gained was significant.

Off I trotted up to the library, I sat on the chair outside in the street and looked up the Bendigo bank on my phone to see if there was one in the area. Yep, up the road round the corner and in the next block. Ohhh, I suppose I should walk it I need the exercise and it was such a drama trying to find a car park. Off I trot/stagger opening a new account with them.

All these incidents might seem insignificant however when feeling vulnerable and sensitive to only the most minor obstacles is like climbing a huge mountain.

Although feeling better this morning I was still a bit flat, however I have my counsellor phoning today hopefully she can put things into perspective for me. I think I'm feeling a bit lost, not sure what to do or where to go, do I get a part time job, if I do where am I going to live, I must be out of here by February when Simone and family get back. *If I buy a place further away out of Brisbane then I need enough money left to survive till I qualify for the pension, a few years off yet, although it is more than I receive now. Hence my quandary which way do I jump.*

I love my Sunday volunteering at the opportunity shop, very up market shop where designers donate clothing to us, these are brand new clothes from their designer studios and the rest of the clothes and oddments are donations. As we get many books donated, Kate has been selecting books for me to read, again the angels are helping pick the books as each one seems to lead on from the next. I find it absolutely incredible and I'm grateful. We meet many nice people and now have regular customers. We both get a lot out of it, especially me, from our Sunday volunteering, great company, lovely honest people, and we were helping others.

Back to the next-door neighbours. As we would go in and out of our respective homes, we would have the occasional courteous hello and how long are Simone and kids away for, I must be enjoying the quiet with them gone, as they were. Ha Ha.

I was mowing the tiny strip of lawn out the front of the house, though I'd shut the back glass door, Simone's dog could repeatedly push on the doors to open them, I had closed the side door from the garage to the shed, the roller door on the shed was up only a fraction. It was enough for the dog (Simone's America Staffy) to push the doors open and get out under the roller door. I yelled at him to get back inside, but he spotted this guy with two dogs walking down the middle of the road. Simone's dog loves kids and people, he has one of the children (5-year-old, daughter of girl also renting Simone's place with me) telling him what to do, sit, stand etc and lying on top of him, but he hates other dogs.

This guy had a massive German Shephard and what looked like a whippet cross. The dog fight was on in the middle of the road. I was frantically trying to get hold of the dogs' collar, each time I got closer this guy would pull on his German Shepherds lead and Simone's dog would move. Neighbours came out from everywhere, Ian from next door came and it was when this guy fell heavily on the road that we were able to get hold of Simone's dogs' collar and pull the 2 dogs apart. This guy had put his hand between the dogs trying to stop them - it beggars' belief, why would anyone would do that. Unfortunately, we found out later that he was bitten, we think by his own dog. The other dog (whipper) got out of his collar and bolted off home. One of the neighbours took the German Shephard to the vet on the corner of our street and Ian and I took Simone's dog inside and out the back into the pool enclosure. This guy was bleeding from his hand, Lola cleaned it up and gave him a glass of water, I thought the bleed was from the fall on the road. Another neighbour's carpenter from across the road, took this guy to the local Dr, who then apparently advised him to go to hospital as he would need stitches, I found out later.

I phoned the vet, and the German Shepard only had a puncture wound in his ear and was given antibiotics and went home. Simone's dog had puncture wounds and blood over his shoulders and neck, Fortunately I took photos with my phone. I was completely shaken, Lola told me later she was worried I would pass out, I didn't look good.

After it all I phoned my counsellor and then phoned and left a message for Simone to phone me. They were in WA, travelling and having a great time, I was envious but happy for them. Finally, Simone phones, I tell her the events of the day, she takes it all in and then hangs up, has to consult with husband. They contacted me asking for pics of Simone's dog, did I take any, Not frickin stupid, of course I took pics and wrote down everything that happened. They wanted the dog taken to the vets to get checked out, 'I'm not taking him,' I'd been through enough, they arranged for a friend to pick the dog up and take him to another vet, different vet to the one the German Shephard was taken. Could I please wash the dog so that he was clean, I did.

Next thing the Brisbane City Council turn up in uniform asking me to make a statement, I was that shaken up I asked them to come back the next day. Which they did and I felt better and more able to cope after the trauma of the day before. There will be a fine as the dog was under my control $287.00, did I want to pay now or have it sent thru the post. 'Send it thru the post please.'

Simone's husband phoned with details of who is picking up the dog and taking him to the vet and back. After the dog was seen by the vet, he phones back later to say nothing wrong with the dog they had also asked the vet to check the dog for the skin allergy the dog had had before they left. The vet reported that the dog was in good health, only requiring a course of antibiotics as a precaution from the other dogs' bites. Then he said the guy could sue and could need physio for years.

Simone texts, I have to pay half the cost for everything, both vet bills and any hospital cost for this guy etc. Hmmm, this is coming from the husband I felt.

I'm still waiting for the fine to come thru the mail which I'm happy to pay. But I will not pay for both vet bills or anything else. I haven't told Simone that yet, as things feel as though they are already very strained. Eventually Simone did ask how I was.

Neighbours have been brilliant, Lola said all the people in the street were on my side, not sure there were sides but nice to know I have their support.

The neighbour across the road who Simone and husband get along with really well, Michelle, did phone as soon as they heard. A few days later I was at the Dr's, figured I needed some sleeping tablets as the trauma had set me off again and I was back to square one. Michelle spotted me there and came over to see how I was, she said she thought it would put me back a bit, commenting that I had been going well. Anyway, she said it was Simone and husband's dog and they should pay the bills, not my problem she said, I need to look after myself. Which was nice. She said they were lucky to have me looking after the dog as "do you know how much it would cost them," I said "funny thing you should mention that, I looked it up on line and the average fee for looking after a dog overnight was $44 minimum." I am pretty certain this has got back to Simone and husband as I haven't heard a word from them since. And I am still paying rent.

As my counsellor said, some things will happen that are going to test me, well they have. And I'm finally learning to listen to my Angels or inner self. I hope that I'm shown the way, but as I keep saying I really needed to learn patience, and this is all teaching me patience. I'm finally catching on.

I found a great place to learn patience is at a doctor's surgery, waiting to see your doctor/specialist. It becomes quite relaxing after a while, a good time to either think or play card games on your phone.

Now you have the details of what my experiences have been the last month, there have been some lovely moments where I've met lovely people, that I cherish and I'm grateful for.

I've rambled on a bit but it felt good to get it out into print, I appreciate, and I'm grateful to all the fantastic people in my life, you especially, and thank you for being there and supporting me. I also appreciate the offer of a roof over my head, might take you up on that, we'll see what life brings me this next month.

Take care of yourself and I certainly hope your operation is a great success. If I could get up there I would, but I gave my word to Simone when she left that I would look after the dog while they were away (saves them paying for kennel etc). I hope that I have a place before they return in January/February, I want to get out of here.

I also made a commitment to visit all my school friends in Feb/March. That's a while off yet.

Much love, Bobbin

To Bobbin
Well, you have really been in the wars, haven't you.
My gosh, an out of the frying pan and into the fire story – I'm absolutely blown away.

You are one of the bravest and most intelligent people I have ever known. All I can say is, keep on keeping on. How you have dealt with the past few weeks and months, is brilliant and it makes me feel like a wimp, when I complain about any of my troubles.
Bubbles

Hi Bubbles

The day you responded I received the fine from the Council for the dog being unattended, as they called it. I went to the post office and paid it immediately. I didn't want any bad Karma. Simone and husband can pay the vet bills, that is their choice as is having the dog put down.

I had been feeling down for a week, thank God for my counsellor, as no matter how I'm feeling she puts things into perspective for me. She listens and then places context around everything. She was expecting me to be down and sort of hit rock bottom, apparently, it's normal, and I'm perfectly normal!! Good to know, actually it's reassuring to know that most people go through challenges hopefully not as dramatic as these? I feel these carry more emotional challenge than anything.

Some friends wanted me to stay in Brisbane, and for years I always accommodated other people's thoughts and feelings. I'm a slow learner but now I'm starting to say no and do what's right for me. A very strange feeling indeed to put yourself first, it's taken me a while but I think I'm slowly getting there.

When I start to look at houses for sale again, I'll include areas further north, I heard from Vince (my eldest son) for the very first time since February. It seems we both crossed lines of understanding last time we spoke, never mind, it was really good to talk to him again.

Out of all the kids, Kai phones me weekly to see how I'm going, I feel our relationship is growing ever stronger, and I'm appreciative of his phone calls and touching base with how life is treating him along with updates on his partner and his son.

Take care Bubbles, I'll certainly try to get up there as soon as I can.

Hi Hon,
It broke my heart to know what happened and what it has done to your relationship with Simone and family. This will stay with you forever, and will colour your life for quite a while.

What can I say, nothing I guess except to reiterate my love for.

I know that people want you to stay in Brisbane, as you are a really good friend and I have to say, you would have gone a lot further in your career, without you know who being a ball and chain around your ankle. Thank Heavens you're shot of him and can live your life as you want, without having him trying to control you. The reason I haven't asked you to stay forever with me, even though it would be nice, is because I know you want and need to live your life as you wish for a change. I'm proud of you for taking your own life into your hands.

What a bugger that you had to pay a fine due to Simone's dog attacking another dog. Speaking of dogs, Toast is fine after his op for prostate cancer. His bark has turned squeaky now. It is funny- he sounds like a one of those squeaky kid's toys.

As you say, you are independent and no-one male or female has a right to try and control you.

Love you and take care.

Bubbles

Hi Bobbin

Getting your life back together, will take a while, after experiencing many years of being controlled by a narcissist; they are masters at training people to believe that they are worthless and stupid. I have mentioned to you before, it starts with small things and builds up to the stage where you can't, or at least are not allowed, to make a decision for yourself. Remember, 'The journey of a thousand miles, starts with the first step' I know that you are going to make that journey and one day would not even piddle on him if he were on fire. You are your own person now.

Glad that you are doing well in the new job. I knew you would: Experience, good personality, and good management skills. You have the lot, everything needed to do the job.

Glad you are heading off for a break, and meeting up with your old school friends. It will be wonderful. As you say, you may not recognise each other, but that will be part of the fun. Isolated? is that because his bloody Lordship kept you away from them? Narcissistic A.. H... that he is.

It will be great to catch up with your brother too. It must be quite a while since you have seen him.

Enjoy your holiday.

Hugs, Bubbles

Many years ago, I was told that if you could count your true friends on one hand then you are truly fortunate. Where would we be without our friends. Even though I had lost contact a few years ago, Bubbles has been a true friend for over 30 years. I was fortunate and grateful we made contact again.

Friends are the most fantastic support, you can talk with them or text and email them with all your woes, it helps to get it out of your system. And they respond with supportive comments, love and sometimes suggestions for moving forward, which really is reiterating what you and they already know about you. This communication is like an unwritten / unspoken law that friends have in supporting each other.

The above provides you with some idea of the few instances that I had, along with the tremendous support I was fortunate enough to have from my longtime friend.

Following the trauma over the incident with Simone's dog I found it difficult to stay in the house, I moved in with my girlfriend's daughter Carol. Although Carol said she did not want any rent, I paid her all the same, in cash.

Carol was separated from her husband and had a disabled son, and although she had been apart from her husband for more than a few years Carol was still very bitter and angry with the world, hating her job, her financial predicament, the list goes on. Over the following months Carol and I settled into a routine. As Carol had no car and was relying on public transport, I would drive them around wherever they needed either grocery shopping or outings.

It was on my last day of holidays in Victoria catching up with Renee and other old school friends Carol sent me a text asking me to move out. It certainly came as a shock, she stated she was not happy that I was on a holiday, and was telling me what I should and should not do with my life – that I should sell my car and what sort of property to purchase, etc. While I really appreciated Carol providing me with a room for a couple of months, her timing could have been better!

I flew back to Queensland the next day, went to work the day after having a meeting first with my manager. I was then advised they were not continuing with the position; it was a new position in the region and they were completing another restructure. It kept getting better. I received my letter; on my separation certificate they recorded that I had resigned. Another slap in the face – wet fish moment.

The priority was to find a place to live, I contacted Kai and Natt, Natt offered me a roof over my head, I could stay with them for a short time. Natt drove down and helped me to move my belongings back to her and Kai's place on the Sunshine Coast while I figured things out.

I had a knee injury from a DV incident a few years previously that I had been coping with however while I was at Kai's I knelt on my knee and injured it further. I was already on the waiting list for a knee replacement, MRI scan showed tendons in knee were seriously torn. Natt took me to the hospital yet they could not do anything only to suggest that perhaps I go private and pay for the surgery. Not cheap when you do not have any insurance. More wet fish.

I phoned my brother in Victoria; he said it sounded like I need a fresh start. He had a holiday house down on the south coast, this would give me time to think. A few days later I made the decision to move to Victoria. I was over these wet fish moments I needed time to gather my thoughts, to have some time out, find some space and time on my own to reflect and gain some strength back.

Sometimes we have to get out of our comfort zone and go into the wilderness, follow our instinct. What we discover will be ourselves, it will be a wonderful experience.

Kai helped me pack a few of my items into the car and I began my journey down to Victoria. On my first stop in Queensland, I was not feeling well when I completed a rapid antigen test (RAT). Fortunately, I had a few kits on me. Great – I tested positive to Covid 19 – what a parting gift from Queensland. On the bright side, at least I was isolated while I was driving on my own. It took me more than a few days of driving, mainly due to not feeling 100 per cent, plus I didn't want to have an accident, as I tired easily. By the time I reach the Victorian border, I had fully recovered and the RAT test indicated I was clear. This was a welcome result as I didn't want to pass Covid 19 on to my brother.

Life brings us many twists and turns. What is important is how we react and handle these. Sometimes we do not handle them too well and we learn from that; other times we do cope okay with the tough times. They all serve to help us grow and, more importantly, make us stronger. They shape us, although at the time that is the last thing on our mind. The thought usually goes along the line of 'What now, when will this ever stop?'

It is going through these experiences that not only makes us stronger but we start to realise we have this inner strength, where we have everything we need within ourselves to deal with life's challenges.

PART TWO

*During my first eighteen months out and away from being controlled I was discovering some of the different lollies in the lolly shop. I explored the world of journalling further. This helped me grow and learn how to live life again.
I hope some of these learnings and experiences
I developed also help you on your journey.*

CHAPTER SIX

NAVIGATING OUR WAY

This chapter encompasses the conditions of how I forged my way forward and kept going via affirmations, journalling and self-reflections.

As mentioned, when I first escaped, I commenced writing everything down that occurred each day. There were many reasons for this. Capturing the progress, or lack of it, each day. Recording His actions towards me, be it text or emails, sometimes communicating via the children. As I mentioned in part one, I had made it clear to the children that I did not want them caught up in the break up and forced to take sides.

Anyone that tells you, 'It'll be okay, don't worry about it, it'll blow over,' has no idea, and no matter how well meaning they might be, most people who have not been through such a traumatic event will not understand, no matter how you explain it or what events you relate to help them understand they will never get it. And that is a good thing. Be forever grateful that they have not had such a horrific experience. After a while we realise it is not worth even trying to explain the events or the trauma to them; not only will it upset them but they do not really need to know, as they will never fully understand.

It is only by working through these difficult times ourself with the help of counsellors that the situation will change for us, our feelings and emotional state. There is much change that we must go through and navigate on our way through the door to the other side. It is not an easy journey, do not get me wrong. It is hard work, but if we remain persistent, we will get there.

Sure, as we escape and find our way, there is a need to talk about what happened. We ask, why me! Why was I so wronged? What did I ever do to deserve this? I am no good. I am useless, ugly. You could go on and on, but this is a process. You are not the only one who has been through it, although you feel like it at the time. One needs to work through the process of reflection and letting go. It helps to get it out of our system. Most important is not to compare yourself to others this is <u>not</u> a state we want to be in or get into. One of my girlfriends told me: 'You are your own wonderful self.' This made me feel humbled, to think that a friend thought this of me. It made me sit, reflect, and appreciate all that I had, great friends and great support and, most importantly, I was alive.

When I escaped, in those first few weeks/months it was extremely hard to:

- *Know what I wanted* - to feel safe is enough.
- *To know what am I going to do, what are my plans?* – no idea yet, my mind is running through many scenarios.

- *Who can I trust* – this one is hard, as everyone takes a different perspective and you lose family and friends along the way.

We need to learn to be not only resilient but to have tenacity.

Quite often as a survivor of rape we adopt the attitude that we are at fault, we make ourselves responsible for all kinds of things. I learnt that blaming ourselves does not help us recover. But the feeling of being defiled, dirty, shameful I could go on and on, but these feelings take time to recover from. Also impacting these feelings is how others react. It is hard enough to have to say you have been raped, let alone cope with the reactions of others, as this can be equally as soul destroying. This is a traumatic experience. Nonetheless the trauma does not define us. It is only one part of our journey.

Journalling proved useful to keep track of the events in order to advise my solicitor. Also, I used it as a reflection to help me to grow to understand this new journey I was on.

Through my journalling listing the tasks I wanted to achieve for the day, the tasks started with going for a walk, going down the street to do the grocery shopping. Writing down these tasks helped me. I then expanded on this to start setting some goals, again to keep my mind occupied and focused.

To a person who has never experienced coercive control or abuse of any kind these seemingly minor tasks appear insignificant. However, each task is enormous for those of us coming out of the situation and finding our own way. At the end of each day, I would write down a minimum of three things that I was grateful for. Being grateful for even the tiniest of events helps us on our journey.

Within your journal, the written words need to be beautiful and precious to you, your words being your thoughts and feelings. They are to capture each precious moment, be it good or not so good.

You are a wonderful, precious person; we all are. Journalling helps us to let our emotions out. You don't have to carry feelings of being alone anymore, as your journal becomes your best friend. Capture every moment, cherish it, and as you reflect upon your writing, within you, you will gain great insight, awareness, wisdom, and strength. This growth will encourage you on your journey in life. The words you write will inspire your soul.

Research indicates that keeping 'a diary helps to make sense of unorganised information, and helps us reach our goals more quickly and easily'. I can definitely attest to this. It helps us in 'understanding and dealing with the crisis and the changes happening in our lives.' The practice of journalling can help lead us to changing our cognitive thinking. We can then work at 'shifting traumatic events into turning points and opportunities.' [26]

It is important for us to have our goals, write them down, really think about what goals we want. Make them small initially, then let them grow as you grow. You will be surprised at how far you have travelled along the journey in a very short time. If you do not want to follow that goal you wrote down, then that is okay. Make a comment below your notation that you no longer wish to chase this goal (it might have been too adventurous at the time); you never know, you might come back to it. I have done this a few times. It's important to ensure that at the time, your goals are achievable. Don't stretch yourself too far in trying to achieve these goals. You have enough to cope with without having to handle more pressure.

As I said, I found setting tasks and goals kept me focused. After a while it becomes very satisfying, being able to look back and see what I have achieved. As I mentioned earlier, my first goal was walking, how far I would walk each day. I picked landmarks to walk to along the foreshore each week. I first set the goal of walking to the lighthouse park. After reaching that goal each day of the week, I then set to walking past the park and halfway towards the local swimming pool. I would set a marker in my mind and that became the objective for that week. It wasn't until my knee finally collapsed that I had to change my goal. Something to be taken up later after the operation to repair my knee.

After a few months, I joined the local library, and asked where the spiritual and self-help books might be located. I have always been drawn to this area.

I learnt much from reading the books that came my way. I started another journal. This was to capture phrases or paragraphs that resonated with me. I felt the words were important; they meant something. These words helped me grow on my new journey. It is like when you meet people for the first time. It might be that something in them reminds you of yourself, or you feel you would like to know them better. Go with the flow.

There are many encouraging comments that started me on my reading journey, and others that had similar connotations which I used to start a scrapbook. What I found interesting was that each book I selected seemed to flow on from the previous one, even the books that friends gave me. In selecting books, I had no plan; I went with my gut feeling and where my hand touched.

You might feel yourself being bombarded with questions and having to make snap decisions, but you feel confused, as you are learning to cope with being out on your own. It helps for each incident or event to focus on the solution not the problem. Additionally, to recognise that a problem is something you have, and not something you are.

Part of what gives us the will to live is being able to imagine a future for ourselves. We need to engage in our emotions, and there is something quite special about journalling that allows us to reach into our deepest self. Life has many ebbs and flows. We need to be adaptable as things twist and turn. We cannot make our dreams too rigid or immobile, as life constantly changes and unexpected things happen which we need to address. It is then that we can choose to incorporate what we want into our lives.

Challenges will continue to come our way. They are a test for us; through them we discover how we work on each one individually, we are learning to cope one step at a time, and believe me, it does make you stronger. The challenges that do come our way in life would not appear if we couldn't cope; it's a growing experience in our journey. I continued to reflect on this, as I find it is a great reminder, bringing me back to the process. We learn and grow strong from all these life experiences. If you think about it, there is always a way.

It's important to remember to take small chunks, or 'little bites' as I have referred to it. 'It is a journey not a sprint'. These words kept echoing in my mind.

There is much we need to consider and be aware of as we move forward. It can get confusing; as I have said our goals may change or we may find that the things we are doing to reach them are not working – this does happen. It is then that we need to reset and go with the flow for a while.

These challenges might be taking us in a new direction and we need to be able to adjust as we go. The strange yet interesting thing is that although we need a goal to keep us going, it is not in achieving the goal that the real satisfaction and happiness lies, but rather in the journey towards it – the focus, commitment and purpose that having a goal provides. It's learning to enjoy what we do that brings real fulfillment. Wealth, power, and fame do not make people happy. But allow yourself to take stock of what you have achieved; do not deny yourself the satisfaction of reaching your goals. Stop and take stock.

The consequences of not living our life according to our true self can begin to eat away at us; we lose our sense of worth, lose who we really are. It takes nerve and an inner strength, one drawn from our core, to go out on our own, to be different. You can do it; others have made it. And I am finding that I also am managing to navigate my way through these feelings and thoughts. Once we get over the worry and feeling of being different, of muddling our way out of DV and of taking life into our own hands, we begin to feel much better within ourselves. Sure, the critics will always be there. So what? That is their problem, do not make it yours. I've learnt not to make it mine. And being our own true self is the greatest feeling. It allows us to look at how far we have come. When we look at all the little bites we have made and put them all together, the achievements they add up to will surprise us, and provide us with the confidence to keep going.

After all, this is our life, not anyone else's. Be true to who you are.

At this point I feel it is important to remind ourselves why we are here. Let us look at this. I would like to take you through some specific and interesting facts. Research has identified that 'non-fatal strangulation is a well-known precipice for the escalation of violence in domestic relationships. Researchers noted that non-fatal strangulation is a strong indicator of future risk for serious harm and the death of a victim, with the risk of becoming an attempted homicide victim increasing by 700 per cent, and the risk of becoming a homicide victim increasing by 800 per cent'. [15]

Before I made my escape, thoughts of trying to ascertain which is worse, the physical or verbal abuse, filled me. There really is no difference; it's all violence. The physical scars heal, the emotional/verbal abuses are unseen these are significantly more difficult to deal with. When you're experiencing fear, you are not facing your fear, it can hold you back from enjoying life to the fullest. Removing yourself from fear, and pressing forward with life is much better than going back or remaining in the same situation. It was only after I escaped that I realised I needed to learn to confront and conquer my fears.

There are phrases which resonate, 'Let your eyes look right on, and let your gaze be straight before you.' Proverbs 4:25.

As I reflected in chapter four, in life you don't go back to the past to see if it still hurts, the pain of yesterday motivations our strength for today. [12]

Don't look down in discouragement or despair, and don't look back; I hold the attitude of been there, done that, not going back. Look ahead, we will learn, grow, and realise our dreams. Without doubt it is tough, but it is a very rewarding experience as we learn to know and treasure ourselves. Serenity shall be ours.

I came across a reference to a word which was broken down in a way that struck me, as I did not necessarily think of it this way.

Intimacy = into me see 13

Most of us are afraid that if people really get to know us intimately, they may not like us or will be shocked by the truth they see. I like this break down of this word intimacy. If we want intimacy, we must be willing to really let people see into us, and we must be willing to see into them. Getting to know people intimately takes time, understanding and a willingness to be deeply honest. True closeness can only be experienced when we respect one another's differences.

Trust is crucial to any bond between individuals; it inspires every human interaction. Trust, at its core, means being emotionally open, to let yourself be seen and known for who you truly are. 18

I openly trust people I meet; this feels good as we both find our way, either in friendship or any other relationship. Maybe because in my marriage to Him there was never any talk, never anything real. I would stay mute as any conversation would only involve my being ridiculed, being put down, abused, I could go on.

One memorable experience I had was when talking to an old friend; I felt unusually relaxed and opened myself to trust implicitly; the trust was reciprocated, this friend opening up freely to me I was blown away, near speechless, this was a lovely experience. The things we talked about were like no other I had ever expressed to anyone before. Sharing in mutual trust, and knowing our conversations were our own, paved the way.

Hence, when I say we place our trust in someone close, it should never be betrayed.

'Trust' comes from the heart, betray it, and 'Trust never returns.'

We are all responsible for making our own choices, but remember, so is everyone else. The coercive control that many of us have endured has no place in our lives. No one has the right to exert control over another. It's important to have the capacity to make our own choices and feel free to do so.

When we set about making any changes, it pays to bear in mind that these changes don't happen overnight. As we leave an abusive relationship, the healing takes time and considerable work in all aspects of our life, but we all find that in changing our cognitive thinking, in choosing our own attitude to a given set of circumstances, and in choosing our own way, the change becomes easier. When everything around us becomes overwhelming and feels like it's out of control, break it down into little bites. Be your true self, as within all of us there is strength. The reward at the end is worth it.

Each one of us must come to terms with our own individual challenges and to learn to find our own happiness within, whatever the situation. Remain upbeat and positive in the face of difficulties. And keep in mind that there is 'more than one way to skin a cat,' look for that 'silver lining'. Remember to stop, pause, smell the roses, and appreciate all that we have achieved to date, no matter how small. And always but always be thankful, grateful for everyone and everything that has come our way. Do not bother looking back – *been there, done that* – there is no going back. Yesterday has gone and we cannot change it now. Look forward and stay happy, no matter what the difficulty.

Take one day at a time. Yes, we plan for our future, but we do not live our future in the present moment, do not let it consume us. Live each moment in the here and now, look for the silver linings, look for the fun and the positives in each moment. Work through the hurdles, as they are character building. Although at the time we are going through our trauma and working our way out it does not feel much like it, it does build strength and character.

Sometimes firsthand knowledge of sitting in our misery could be the incentive we need to master our own happiness, if we want to change the way we feel. I like Alexander Graham Bell's famous statement 'When one door closes, another opens.' I am sure we have all been told this at one stage or another. The closing signaling the end of a stage in our life, and the opening of another brings about new beginnings as we continue on our endeavors, and move forward. [20]

When we feel uncertain or when events in our lives make us feel insecure or unsafe, the small rituals we practise each day can provide us with a valuable sense of stability. Remember, we always have a choice, and the choice is ours to make not someone else's. There will be wet fish moments, they are our challenges, don't let them rule you by taking them personally, utilise your inner strength. Sure, there will be mistakes but these are our opportunities to learn and grow. We always have the choice of how to handle these challenges, break it down, take little bites and move in the direction of your choosing.

For me, initially, it was difficult not to take things personally. When you've experienced coercive control, you are used to being blamed, verbally abused, having to cope with severe criticism, for being at fault for anything and everything. You are also isolated, have no friends to call on or to talk to about what you're going through. You tend to take everything to heart, to take it personally. It really takes tenacity and an even stronger attitude to overcome these emotions. It's very hard to stand and fight these challenges, but when I was going through this, I was determined to see it through; I was finding my inner strength. There was more to life and I wanted to explore it. Call me bull headed or determined, but I was going to find my way forward out of this.

When we go through any sort of crisis, feelings of shock, believe it or not, helps to cushion the initial impact. When we experience a crisis from any sudden and unusual event our immediate reaction is disbelief. As the onslaught continues, and we realise this is real, it is actually happening, we are not imagining it. Our immediate reaction is that of survival. Survival being a very real and strong emotion, survival is the paramount need during any immediate crisis. We have a need to escape to avoid further attack, we don't want any further attention drawn to us. Then we start to withdraw, breaking off any contact with our support network of family or friends. Its feelings of humiliation, disbelief, and shame we might even feel embarrassed for not being able to think clearly while the crisis was happening. It's afterwards when we try to process all these mixtures of emotions that the fear hits us. As a victim, we might experience anger as we work through our recovery, as we try to wrestle with living again. Our body copes in mysterious ways when trying to process the trauma, trying to come to grips with life.

Then compound this with a life of being manipulated and isolated by a narcissist!

It is important to remember to breathe and remove all the negatives, to stop putting ourselves down. We are all wonderful individuals; we all need to find ourselves again. By being open we can find who we really are; this is truly courageous. It's crucial to believe in yourself. We can all do it, there is no time limit on achieving this. Most of us have similar wishes in life, to belong, be connected, to experience love and happiness. Do not give up when the challenges come. Stop, take a breath, and break what you're dealing with down into little bites. Let life take you on this journey.

I continue to reiterate the importance of journalling each day, as it helps us through the process. I always find when I write something down that I've released it from within, thereby allowing me to move forward.

With the affirmations that I obtained through cards and/or little books, I found that writing them down each day in my journal, not only helped me to understand and digest each affirmation, but it became mine for that day to guide me.

Nevertheless, the feeling of being out of control and powerless can be very demoralising. We must always remind ourselves of what is in our control and what is not. We need to learn to discard the things that are not in our control. Why put ourselves through the stress and worry? After all, what is the end game? 'Be persistent and be resilient.' [33]

Again, we are governed by our thoughts. Think about your thoughts. Be careful about your thoughts, stop criticising or berating yourself, be kind to yourself. Don't go back over those feelings and thoughts of helplessness, as these thoughts have potential to destroy us, restricting us from moving forward. Stay positive, always look for the good in every aspect of life, and delight and be thankful for the positives that you experience.

Although not happening quite as often now, I find some triggers take me back. This is when I must apply more effort into controlling my thoughts, turning them into positives. Do not look back; you are not going that way. Around the corner there are better things waiting.

As I've stated throughout, I found journalling the most rewarding, thing for me to do. Everyone has a different way. You will know what suits you, do not worry if you do not journal. Your way will come to you. I found that once I wrote it down, I could move on, only looking back occasionally to reflect on how far I have come and what I have learnt along the way. This really helped me, and, it also enabled me to sleep, as I did not have it playing on my mind. As I said previously, once written down it was out of me and I could reflect on it later. I felt free to stop spiraling in the same trauma, around and around. I felt free to move forward, to laugh and enjoy the company and support of others. F...ing easier said than done, though. This really does take tenacity, as it certainly does take time and that is where patience comes in. Learn to be patient with yourself, to treat yourself with kindness, with kid gloves. Get into the garden or create something. Find a project, or help others. I went volunteering in an opportunity shop and it was the best time. I was helping a good cause, helping those clients that need more support than I, telling stories of happy experiences in life, in my case this was often travels and places seen. I not only worked with great people but met great people, all of a kindred spirit. If volunteering is not your thing, you could go and sit in a park under a lovely tree, daydream and listen to nature and the birds. Nothing wrong with that, good for the soul.

Once we have felt and moved through our uncomfortable feelings, we will sense that we have learnt from some of this but, most importantly, we have also become stronger within ourselves. This is our life and although we do not always know where we are going straight off the bat (I did not), through the decisions we make doors open and life changes, even if challenges come to us from the least expected places at times. Learn to accept and go with it, as we do not know where it is going to take us. But if it does not feel comfortable or right, move away. Be gracious and say thank you, but this is not for me, I need another path.

A new journey is ready to begin. A new door is waiting to open to you. Follow the path of the bold. Every time you think you cannot move forward, review your journal, your goals, and see how far you have come. Take a moment to appreciate your strength, that you've had the tenacity to move forward with your life. It is not so much the attainment of our goals as it is the process of striving after goals – that is growth – that brings happiness. When we are feeling happy, we are more likely to take risks, reach out to others and expose ourself to rejection and failure. When feeling unhappy, one feels defensive, touchy, and self-conscious.

Do not be bound by fear of failure. A life driven by love is preferable to a life driven by greed. Be bold and express your feelings; affirmations help. As I wrote them up each morning I would breathe with intention, stilling the mind, always trying to let go. By letting go of the tensions and trusting my inner self, I found that glow within, this can be both confronting but comforting. It is important not to be too hard on ourselves. Surrender can bring happiness.

Remember 'Take Little Bites.'

CHAPTER SEVEN

MAKING ROOM WITHIN OURSELVES

Some of the morals and personal traits my mum taught me when I was young were independence and self-control; they were very useful traits to have. You might ask why, when I left home to marry, I said to Mum, 'I'm a survivor.'

I lost my father when I was 13, mum and I had always been more like sisters than mother and daughter. We could talk about anything, - well mostly. It was quiet an adjustment when Dad passed away, a lot of changes for us all. I had to step up and help mum, and grew up very quickly, dealing with accountants and solicitors was a steep learning curve for me.

Having a special bond like mum and I had, I could feel that mum was really concerned for me, she once said to me, your marrying the person not the family. My words to mum of being a survivor came from deep within me, I knew within my heart of hearts no matter what came my way I would survive. Little did I know how true these words were, and how they would come to fruition.

Sad to say, in my senior years at school didn't feel anyone was interested in me or wanted to be with me. I was lonely. When attention was given, I took it, even when it was the wrong type of attention.

Touch is an important feeling for me. Over the years to never feel a partner give any affectionate touch adds to the numbness you feel when getting abused. I spiralled down even further into the depths; not of despair, moreover a void of darkness. Under His control friends were taken from me, and even those friends that remained were confined to his control. It was only a very few people that I've been able to maintain contact with over the years, and even then, I couldn't talk to them about what I was going through, my feeling of shame was so great. All I could do was react, survive, second guess everything, and protect and care for my children draining my energy immeasurably. Resilience and tenacity were my keys to positive change.

Narcissist and trauma

Bubbles had always picked it; she had sensed that He was a narcissist. I do not always see these things; I suppose because I always choose to look for the good in each person, to look for the silver lining. I am here to tell you that there is not always a silver lining. Sometimes you need to go beyond the cloud to find the light, and sometimes there is no light.

Those of us who have experienced life living with narcissists know how they tend to be self-centered, self-obsessed, and less likely to make sacrifices for others. Studies have revealed this to be true, as dominant partners are less prepared to grant to their spouses' requests and more likely to attack with aggressive comments. Dominant people are less willing to indulge in 'give and take,' especially with those over whom they believe they have greater standing. It has become more widespread that the dominant person rules through fear, rather than love.

A person who has experienced an event that is outside the range of usual human experience, one that would be markedly distressing to almost anyone, can be defined as having Post Traumatic Stress Disorder (PTSD). Being the victim of a personal disaster such as a violent crime, assault, or rape, and/or having a life-threatening experience, all potentially contribute to PTSD.

When we live a life that is not completely ours, or we are living in trauma, we will never be happy, contented, or joyful. We could feel responsible for other people's feelings or feel it's difficult to say no. We fear rejection and abandonment and compromise our values or sacrifice our own happiness and well-being for others. We lose our way and have trouble setting or reinforcing boundaries. Our feelings and emotions become difficult to express.

Over eighteen months, following my escape, at every location I moved to I sought out various doctors regarding a variety of ailments, trying to sort out what was wrong. I had terrible bouts of dizziness and felt unsteady on my feet, though as I mentioned previously this was likely due to exhaustion. I was not used to allowing myself time to recover. – Patience again. This dizziness was because of the trauma I experienced. There were other ailments: an upset stomach and stomach cramps, gastro, loss of muscle tone, chest pains and hair loss. Again, I was advised this was all due to the trauma I had endured. Even when I had not told the doctor of my situation, they would ask, and continue to pursue a certain line of questioning in order to find the root cause. In each situation, I had to fess up to being a DV victim, where there was no other medical concern, and they would all conclude these aliments were due to trauma. This is where 'Emily Francis's book, *The Body Talks* really provided me with some understanding of what was going on

Trauma, the gift that keeps on giving!

Living in stress puts out bodies under constant physical strain. It can increase blood pressure, and in turn increasing the risk of heart disease. The immune system is thrown into disorder, making us more susceptible to illness and disease. Living in continual stress the body has no natural dispersal of the stress hormones, this stress remains in the body, causing ailments. A useful technique for dealing with difficult emotions and situations is mindfulness. It can help us feel better and reduce our stress.

We need to learn to loosen the knots within ourselves, to allow ourselves time, and to shine our light. Breathing correctly and focusing on the present moment of our breathe, mindfulness, is how we work through this. Our skin and muscles feel tight, tense, using mindfulness along with massage helps our body relieve the tensions. Concentrate on your breathing and the existing moment, as it does relax the tensions. [19]

When we begin to feel comfortable in opening ourselves again, we invite the spiritual growth that is an ultimate need for each of us. Intimate connections help bring us closer to fulfilling our hearts and achieving feelings of being whole. Not all of us are fortunate enough to experience or find our absolute true love or soul mate. Having experienced a domestic violence situation, one becomes very hesitant to start anew. We become very wary and it is hard to trust. However, once we have found ourselves it becomes easier, as we have diminished the shame, and the traumas, that we have carried, and we have opened our hearts to ourselves and those special to us. We begin cautiously to place our trust, and gradually expose our vulnerabilities. We can only pursue the search for our own soul with a clear and open heart.

We all face fear when we start on something new, but keep going. Confident and courageous people have acquired these personality traits by following their dreams and overcoming failures, and disappointment, by bouncing back time and time again. Persistence is the key. Maybe we cannot get where we want to go by going straight ahead, but remember there are sides and corners and other angles to tackle our goals from (that is, there is more than one way). If at first you don't succeed, try again.

*

What does truth mean to you? Do you live by your truth, or are you afraid of revealing your true self? I've seen people searching for answers, their search was external. And while knowledge attained can be helpful, it's not until we start to search within ourselves that we find our true self along with our answers.

When I was in a toxic relationship all I could do was react, survive, second guess and look after the children whilst I was drained of my own energy.

Now I had to overcome the shame, look for the light and love within myself, not the love I was searching for externally, but actually learning to love myself first. I had to release myself to God, the angels, the elements, and nature for my healing.

If you think this is easy, think again. I've really had to struggle with finding myself, of letting go, and just accepting what comes my way, this in itself is difficult.

I had to rely on my resilience, and tenacity whilst learning, and accepting along the way.

Truth, listening with our heart, being a good observer, listening with our soul, these are the real strengths within. The scenario often used by people who are coming out the other side of a domestic violence situation is of a caterpillar moving through the stages of its life, going into the chrysalis before emerging as a beautiful butterfly. We can all do this using our minds to change our attitude, change our cognitive thinking. Of course, I'm not saying it is an easy road to travel.

It is when we are completely devoid and start our journey to rid ourselves of the past traumatic emotions, when we remove our fear and the outside influences, that we begin to learn and grow. We start to choose how we look at each and every part of our life; we clear out the rubbish in order to start a new life. We need to put those <u>big girl's shoes on</u> and go and grab what we want from life, looking inside each door whether we want to or not. As I said it is not easy no one ever said it was, but good things will and do follow. It is a struggle to turn the ordinary into the not so ordinary, but keep moving forward.

When we manage and begin to overcome our fears, we have the potential within ourselves to achieve anything we want in life. It seems such a long ride when we are coping with challenge and trauma, but it is well worth the effort.

I cannot stress the importance of changing our cognitive thinking, of recognising that it's not the moments of tragedy that define our lives, much as the choices we make to deal with them.

The only boundaries that we have are those that we build and establish for ourselves. This is why it's important to change our cognitive thinking, to be positive, to be optimistic. One important obstacle is to remove our egos, as we tend to drag them around with us every day. Do try to remove your ego; it is hard work but it is very worthwhile. We begin to feel free, open and vulnerable, yes, but we no longer feel held back, or restrained, and we will not feel the fear. Realise that only the ego thinks in terms of superior or inferior. Never give into self-importance. Learn to listen with body, heart, mind and soul.

The power of the present moment is to be free from both the past and the future, to have the flexibility in the moments as they reveal themselves. It's by not allowing our memories to use us. It's okay to use them, but don't let them use us. We need to ascertain what we want to get rid of, and really commit to letting go of the obstacles that are holding us back. To find real solutions, determine what we really want and why, and in doing so we need to be determined, be tenacious.

Analyse the way you view each obstacle you experience; although daunting, determine how you might be able to overcome it by breaking it down into little bites. That way you will find it easier to overcome each individual obstacle you face. If you identify what you truly want, overtime you will find yourself learning how to reach that goal. It's important to recognise that hardship is a universal and inescapable part of life, however we can gain the resilience to enable us to cope.

*

It is a sad fact that the negative things in our lives have a habit of demanding all our attention. We learn at work to set our goals and make them SMART, (specific / measurable / achievable / realistic / time framed). Changing our behaviour affects our feelings and thoughts, as will changing our cognitive thinking shift our behaviour. We all get feelings of being anxious or nervous. This could happen when we have a blind date or meet someone famous. We have a choice; do we go to meet them or not? I had one such experience when I was to meet someone whom I had not seen for many years. My inner feelings were turning me inside out, and were extremely hard to control, yet did I decide not to go? No. I went to meet this person for coffee, and the most unusual calm came over me. Yes, I was extremely nervous, anxious, apprehensive, and excited, yet when the feeling of calm came over me (which surprised me), I could absorb and experience the moment.

Remember change is not a straight trajectory. Sometimes we need to go around a corner instead of straight ahead to get to where we want to be. However, we can make it if we have patience and compassion for ourselves, leading from the heart or simply trusting ourselves to make that decision that is true to the values that we hold close. This can make our lives more fulfilling. Our connections with ourself and others can fuel our enthusiasm for life. It can be a difficult road, with many obstacles, but life is worth it, is it not?

Creating a new habitual path that is as effective as the old familiar path is different for everyone. 'Prioritising consistency over a quick fix is the key to overcoming habits, as is taking your time. On average, research suggests it might take anywhere from 18 to 254 days, contrary to the popular belief that you can break a habit in 21 days.' 23 By taking little bites one small step at a time and putting the new step into practise regularly, we can change to our new habit, and these can be valuable for adopting a new mantra as we move forward from past traumas.

Every one of us has a journey to take. I am no saint, but I knew for my own peace of mind that in order to move on I had to let go of the past. I was damaged, yes, but I had a whole life waiting for me and I'd be damned if I was going to live in the past. 'I will survive, as I am a survivor.'

The further I travel through this journey, the more I am reminded of what Simone had said to me: 'Think where you'll be in two or five years' time.'

It is how we approach life's challenges that makes the difference in how we proceed, and that is not necessarily the same way we might have approached life in the past!

*

Previously I alluded to how the journey we go through in trauma is not dissimilar to a caterpillar which goes into its chrysalis for a while, only to come out as a beautiful butterfly. The growth of the caterpillar into a butterfly takes time. <u>It cannot be rushed or the butterfly will have damaged wings.</u> Take the time to be patient within yourself and remember your heart's deepest desires and dreams. Slow down, and let your fears dissolve. Breathe and reflect. Concentrate on what your heart desires, and what you really want.

Another key trait which I found helpful to support me in my endeavours to find happiness and be confident was, as I indicated earlier, to stop taking things personally. Of course, this is easier said than done sometimes, as the feeling of deep self-criticism is one all of us can experience, although some of us have more self-criticism than others.

Then you have the narcissist who exploits it.

Narcissists are exceptionally good at criticising others, however do not accept criticism themselves, as they only love themselves and feel they can do no wrong.

When a woman is told she is ugly, it stays with her forever. The sentiments expressed here are often true. When someone says something like this to us, it can take quite a bit to work through this and turn it around enabling us to regain confidence in ourselves, as we have had it drained from us on purpose. It takes an enormous amount of effort to change negative cognitive thinking and be able to acknowledge ourselves. I flipped this by thinking about where the comments have come from. Was it from someone who wanted to exert control over me by shaming me? When we break it down and look at it in a different light or from a different angle, little by little we can feel ourselves start to overcome feelings of shame and worthlessness.

When we have been hurt and berated for a very long time, as the case with many domestic violence circumstances, we get used to feelings of self-criticism. For example, continually feeling depressed and down on ourselves, and for some it is a mammoth shift to counter these feelings, depending on what each of us has experienced within domestic violence, and for how long. To get to know, acknowledge and appreciate ourself is sometimes hard to do, but very worthwhile. Like other journeys we must go through, this takes not just resilience but also tenacity.

Turn the criticisms around, think of the source that exasperated and perpetuated the feelings you have been left with. They do not control us anymore. What is it about them that causes them to have to try and put us down and make us feel worthless? Could it be their own insecurities, or are they hiding deeper mental health issues? But ask a narcissist and they will tell you they do not have any problems; in their mind, they are perfect.

CHAPTER EIGHT

LAUGH AND SMILE

A smile needs to be heartfelt; people see through a fake smile.

Have you ever noticed that when you are feeling good, you achieve positive results. Negativity attracts even more negativity. Life is fast, we are all very busy, but if we slow down if only a little and focus on the moments and events in life that we are grateful for, and the moments that make us happy, sometimes that is all it takes for a smile to sneak across your face. Try it; you will be surprised. Like the age old saying goes 'Stop and smell the roses.'

To smile is to show something positive, and will bring you positive things in return. We learn from our mistakes; some of us take longer to learn than others, some have priorities like the provision of care and shelter for the young. But learn from our mistakes we will and we do.

It is a matter of having a positive outlook and, as the saying goes, to respond like 'water off a duck's back' to some of the events that you face. I cannot recall the number of times I resorted to saying this, and I continue to have this outlook, for protection of my inner self as much as anything. I manage to keep upbeat most of the time and I love to be a smiley person, and to bring a smile to others. I had not realised that I stopped smiling, and it soon became a habit. He might have controlled the mood at home by being a pessimist; however, I could smile outside this environment, and share it with others. Smiling is contagious, and even if someone cannot smile back, they are likely to have received the smile internally. It might be the thing that uplifts them in their thinking and helps them to move forward. Remember, we are never too busy to stop and smell the roses or to impart a smile.

I felt I had to fight very hard, both internally and with life's daily challenges, to stay on this journey. I know that escaping from domestic violence and its effects are not easy, not in the slightest. It is hard emotionally, and physically it really takes it out of you, but my hope is that we can all come through wiser, stronger and with bright eyes and smiley faces, looking towards a fulfilling future.

In our acts of kindness for another we bring about an increase in our wellbeing, where we experience positive emotions, and we may even form a new relationship. There is a feeling of satisfaction in helping others, no matter how small the deed such as smiling. Along with having friends, family, and social connections, these contribute to restoring our wellbeing.

'Anyone can make you smile, many people can make you cry, but it takes someone really special to make you smile with tears in your eyes.' – Anonymous

As I mentioned, although I seldom cry, I do, however, break out into hysterical laughter. If I fall and hurt myself, my first reaction is to laugh, even if I am seriously hurt. The last time I fell was when I was on my way to have x-rays on my leg and knee. The pavement was extremely uneven, I mean really bad, and, apparently quite a few people had fallen on this pathway before. Well, you guessed it, I tripped, and face planted into the bricks.

In the past when I had fallen, all I got from Him was abuse at being clumsy and stupid.

But this time, I was grateful to a total stranger who helped me pick up all the beads from my bracelet that had broken, and then helped me to the place where I could have an x-ray. There the nurse cleaned my face, making sure there were no stones or bits of gravel imbedded in my cheek and head. This was some considerable time ago now and, thankfully, I no longer have the tendency to fall. I learnt to pick my feet up, ha ha!

In trying to achieve an attitude in which we always strive to attain the best that we can, there will be times when we stumble and fall, that's okay, we learn from our mistakes. But laughing, especially laughing out loud, can feel fantastic. It feels good when you laugh with such exuberance that you feel your tummy hurt, and you cannot seem to stop. Regain your laugh, you'll be surprised how good it makes you feel.

Remember, a smile needs to be genuine to be heartfelt as others will see straight through a fake smile.

One thing I found to be important is to learn to let go. Some things we have no control over, and it is not worth the head damage to worry about it. Keep blowing those bubbles, learn to let go. Once I stopped trying to control things around me, I was surprised how good I felt. I was more relaxed, free of worry and I noticed that my face relaxed, that I was free to smile again. Initially this did not come easily to me, yet over time, when I found myself laughing and smiling, my face relaxed and it felt good. I could feel the tension dissipate.

It's important for us to have an optimistic and positive outlook in order to help us move forward on our journey.

Tonics for our souls are smiles and laughter.

In life we all need to feel good to be happy and generate more positive emotions, increase the joy, love, pleasure, intimacy and gratitude. It is about feeling good about living the life that is truth for us, it is also about virtue, doing our duty, and living up to expectations we set for ourselves. Both positive and negative thoughts can influence us and impact on our happiness. But having a good laugh and a long sleep can be the best remedies. Worrying only drains today of its joy.

Without a good, whole-hearted laugh, without fun and play, our resilience wains and we lose the ability to keep things in perspective. When people laugh together, they tend to talk and touch more, also they make eye contact more frequently. See how true this is next time you are with friends having a laugh. Laughter is a source of social bonding. To laugh, and be able to make people laugh, is one of life's most attractive and enjoyable qualities in life.

Smiling stimulates brain patterns which reinforce feelings of happiness and optimism. The zygomatic muscle is the smile muscle, the one I have problems with at times. It goes back to when I was a teenager and a new student came to the school I was attending. I instantly had a soft spot for them, but all I could do was say hi and smile whenever we crossed paths. I don't think he ever noticed me, and wasn't at the school long before he moved on. I buried my feelings deep within myself where no one could find them. A long-lost experience, (I couldn't control the zygomatic muscle) but I learnt what a true smile felt like and could do.

The heart can be, the most fragile of all our body parts; the emotions running through our heart can absolutely break us or lift us up to boundless delights. The heart, once lit, and each time it is stimulated, brings many changes to the body one example is the power of a smile: smiling stimulates brain patterns.

Throughout life, my philosophy has always been, 'If you can get one person to smile a day, it has been a great day.' Think of what it is doing to their heart, and yours!

Your smile radiates positive energy, studies indicate that a person that smiles a lot is perceived as being more attractive, sincere, sociable, and competent than someone who does not smile. Happy people are more at ease with themselves, this in turn inspires confidence in others. Notice the difference in your interactions with others when you smile, why? Because we thrive on happiness and sharing our good feelings with others. Like I have said already smiles are contagious and no different to laughter.

CHAPTER NINE

CHANGING OUR OUTLOOK

Have you ever noticed that whatever comes our way, it is usually no more than we can actually handle, even if we don't think so at the time? We learn and grow strong from these life experiences. If you think about it, there is always a way.

It's difficult when we constantly have issues and problems coming at us. Have you ever thought of looking at the problem from a different perspective? As I've suggested earlier, we need to break these down. What is in your control and how can you change your circumstances? Concentrate on one thing you could do to help manage the situation or contribute to solving the problem. Are there any resources you can utilise? Is there an opportunity hiding in this problem that you have yet to consider? With any difficult situation or setback you face, focus on what you can do as opposed to what you can't. Look for effective ways to break the setback down into little bites in order to step towards accomplishing your goal.

After all, this is your life. You need to feel comfortable in your approach, as you tackle each task at your own pace. From personal experience, a common mistake to making life changes is doing too much too fast. I needed to plan small steps towards my goals. This is what life is like; it is lived in tiny steps. Life is made up of tiny events—little bites. Only hindsight can reveal the significant moments in our lives and how they were built upon to make a story.

Taking small Steps: what is one small change in different areas of your life, like your work spaces or your car, perhaps your wardrobe, that you can do today? For example, I finally felt free to choose my own clothes without any condemnation. I purchased the clothes that I liked and felt good wearing and discarded the clothes attached to hostile memories.

That little bite was so significant and helped me to remember that my journey was not a sprint.

When we interrupt an event, it helps us to stop, sit quietly and often enables us to catch our breath. Stopping, for even a moment, can help us to feel clearer and freer. Maybe it is because this offers us time to reflect or brings us back to our breathing to enable us to centre ourselves at our core. When we don't fight the challenges or life itself, and when we sit quietly with our breath and allow the events to flow, this can help us feel clearer and free, giving us time to reflect and enable us to centre ourselves at our core. Letting go, allows our inner self to shine through. That, in itself, relaxes my body. I am then able to follow my intuition. When less overwhelmed by everything, life becomes a little easier to manage.

When we take a break, we no longer live in panic mode and have slowed the fast-paced world of go go go to bring out balance. We find we have time to focus solely on our own needs, but will still need to take little bites. Sure, it does not come easily but, with practice, we are able to gain much more vision. By taking little bites, the things we were putting off or did not feel comfortable tackling become easier to manage.

Taking a break allows us time to reflect, to grow and to accept that we cannot change everything at once, perhaps some things not at all and that it's time to let these things go. It helps us to understand what we need, what we want, what direction we feel comfortable with, and what does not. Listen to your inner self, to your heart. Do not give in to the bullshit. Do your best to feel and speak your truth. Remember, take little bites, one at a time, not all at once.

Sometimes the path we take might not always work out, but what have we lost from trying? It might lead us in what appears to be the wrong direction, but we lost nothing; we still grew and learnt along the way. Take time to regroup and try another tack. It's no biggee; we're alive and breathing. Take that break, allow yourself to relax. Look around with innocent eyes, look at all the things you have. Look at how majestic nature is. Appreciate your support group, friends and family.

Take your time, have trust in yourself and breathe. Look back at how far you have come. Where were you at the beginning of your journey? Take a moment to realise how much stronger you have become. What have you learnt about yourself and others? The bravest people are not those who have no fear, but those who acknowledge the fear, and face it before overcoming it. It's calming to take a regular break to reflect and see how far you have travelled, whether the journey commenced two, three, six or more months ago, or even a year or two ago.

No matter what stage you are at, you still need to take the time to rest and use the time to reflect, maybe to wait for the situation to change. Looking for the inner self is not always easy, but we can develop inner freedom and in turn rise above all the drama. Isn't that something to look forward to?

Throughout all this, remember to be elastic, to look at the situation from different angles. The road is not ever straight. When we remain open, we discover there is more than one way.

Do not wait for the challenges to stop before beginning a new journey, because they won't. Remember, that's part of life. It is all a matter of perspective, about how we break the challenges down, unpack them, taking little bites.

Don't confuse the need to confront the most brutal facts of your reality, with the belief that you will be able to remove them. There have been passages within this book that, as I wrote them, I was pushing myself to reveal feelings I didn't want to revisit. Tears flowed as I wrote the words and paragraphs. However, as I continually reviewed the paragraphs, it became easier. Remaining focused helped me through.

Self-control is the struggle between being impulsive and considering what could be beneficial. It is the ability to control our impulses or emotions to achieve a greater goal. It's all about our cognitive thinking and the need to have focus. A positive outlook inspires us to move forward. We feel satisfaction in moving forward and achieving our goals. Others may admire our effort and ability to work through these hurdles and achieve the outcomes we are looking for. This is what spurs on that ability to realise each achievement.

Throughout the process of leaving my domestic violence situation, I moved into different forms of accommodations depending on my needs at the time. This meant I also changed doctors. As I said in an earlier chapter, each doctor I saw to find out why I was experiencing my various ailments associated them to trauma. 'The muscles simply store what the body has endured throughout this life – this is both great memories as well as traumatic memories.'10

Did you know that 'when we go through any shame, fear, guilt, betrayal or any trauma, it is not only stored in our minds and our brains, but also in our bodies?'10 I found this information about trauma hiding in our muscles enlightening, and the further I investigated this the more I realised how much our body not only stores, but also copes with, regardless of how we think we have hidden our trauma for years. Different feelings can come through when we have exercised a high degree of strength in camouflaging our feelings, be it trauma or perhaps even feelings of affection towards another.

As Emily Francis describes in her book, *The Body Heals Itself*, 'You are a pain in the neck' comes from the 'emotional pains that can store themselves in the neck: stress, pain, tensions, and irritation, all live in the neck. The neck is the most emotional muscle of the entire body it holds trauma of all kinds. Physical trauma such as being chocked, strangled or any violent act, sits in the neck area as a muscle memory. The neck also holds more subtle trauma, such as things you have not said or wished you had not said, the memory of being verbally abused. Not knowing what to do or sticking up for yourself or leaving a situation sits deep within the neck area. Coughing is a form of release, all sadness, shame, guilt, fear, abuse, and pain leaves as you cough from this muscle.' 10

I had an occasion where I went for a remedial massage, I was looking forward to the massage to have all the tension in my back and shoulders massaged out. However, this was different. The guy performing the massage was made aware that I was a DV person but not the circumstances. He asked if I was comfortable having a man conducting the massage. I explained to him that I did not foresee any issues. I informed him of my bursitis and soreness in my knee and right leg. He went to work on my left side, which did not have any issues at all. I thought this strange, however, he was very good and patiently explained how one side of the body interacts with the other side. It was when he asked me to push against him with my left leg and then to push against him with my arms that I fell apart. It took me straight back to being strangled and how I had to push with all my might against his chest with my leg, how I had to push against him with my arms outstretched trying to somehow release his grip from around my neck.

I could not hold back my emotions. I sobbed, having to go through those feelings again. However, it released many of the hidden emotions that I had been bottling up inside. I cried and cried until I explained to the poor man, who had no idea what I had been through, why this was affecting me this way. I was a wreck. And while I appreciated having this come out, I could not go back the next week for a follow-up massage.

*

I called into a crystal shop years ago when I felt I was having difficulty expressing myself at work and I needed to speak up. I bought a ring with a Larimar stone, this being one of the stones representing the throat chakra. It's a lush stone that exudes feelings of relaxation. Larimar is all about those high vibrations that shake fears loose. Although this gem is primarily a throat chakra stone, it also connects to the heart chakra, the third eye chakra and the crown chakra. Dealing with all those upper chakras reminds us how everything is connected. Larimar is about the highest good. Larimar works by bringing balance and harmony to our energies enabling us to achieve overall calm, relaxation and unity within. The properties Larimar possess, provide powers that are both mental and physical. 35 For Larimar, that means speaking our truth without fear. Whether you take this on or not is up to you, of course, each to his or her own.

*

I felt a special connection to Emily Francis' book as I do not and never have been one to show emotions especially through tears. My favourite quote, 'Tears are the physical manifestation of pain leaving the body, the number one most effective way to release serious, deep pains. **Once they are out you cannot put them back in.**' We are advised that when the tears start to flow, we gain the feelings of slowing down, to lessen the pressure, and let the energy be coaxed to flow more freely. To go with the flow. I have never been one to easily cry, in fact I rarely cry, instead I bury my emotions very deep inside where no one can see them.

    I have on a couple of occasions experienced the complete release of letting the tears flow and emptying the emotions out of my body. This happened when I took the journey down the rabbit hole, and again when I had remedial massage and it triggered the trauma of fighting to survive during strangulation. There have been other instances. As everyone is different you will experience your own. I'm not referring to a cry here, but the release of all your emotions, when you are in a very dark place. Emptying out these emotions through uncontrollable tears, where the body shakes is a great release, but we must be able to acknowledge and bring ourselves out of this space. Take note of how you feel after the tears slow and then stop.

Exhausted, yes; pressure relieved, yes; time to rest; yes. But you, 'cannot put the tears back in', can you? The years of pain and shame, guilt, fear, exhaustion—you name it—leave the body. The emotional release is powerful, it might shake you to your core, these moments are life changing. 10

Interestingly, 'We feel anchored when we cannot let go of past traumas, it's through our legs and knees that the emotional tensions hold us back.' 'When we have issues with our knees, we might feel like we are standing in quicksand like it is very hard to lift our feet and move in any direction. This might occur when we are facing big changes in our life or whenever things are changing around us and we do not have much say in it.' In my case, I kept tripping over and falling, usually when I was having difficulty in charting my way through what felt new and daunting. 10

For a long time I could not lift my left leg high enough to independently place my leg into my tights or jeans, or whatever pants I was wearing. I had to lift my leg with my hand. Writing this book and reflecting on my journey since I escaped has helped me immensely. First, I started to notice that I could lift my left leg higher and without assistance, both the height I could lift my leg and foot and the ease with which I could place my foot into my jeans, improved. Another source came from remedial massage, this was very confronting but it assisted me to regain the movement in my left leg (this leg was the culprit that would drag occasionally and causing me to trip and do those face plants onto the bitumen; it was the same knee I had bent against His chest trying to hold Him off while He was strangling me).

I have had surgery to repair all the damage to torn muscles in my right knee due to trauma, which in turn caused a cyst.

Following this earlier DV incident, I always walked with my right foot pointing outwards and had a limp from the pain in my knee. Not only was I suffering from the DV incident where the physical damage was done, but the emotional traumas were also holding me back. [24]

After the operation I grew stronger, and more importantly, over the past year, my ability to cope emotionally and in what I call 'wet fish' moments, through exercising my legs, I was able to walk freely. Walking became a new and pain-free, joy. And I no longer walked with my right foot pointing outwards. When I pointed this out to my specialist on a follow-up visit, he promptly replied, 'This is not from the operation; this is your doing.' That sat me on my backside and it has brought me considerable pleasure.

I love fossicking and taking photos of sea-shells and patterns in the sand. I cannot begin to explain how much I enjoy going for a walk in a park or along the beach now.

Miracles happen each day. Remember where there is breath there is life and a hope that anything is possible. Take a deep breath. You will feel all the better for it and always but always remember to say <u>thank you</u>.

One act of acknowledging yourself is accepting and letting go. Forgiveness will become a vital part of our healing process. As part of this process, 'Forgiveness is the practice of remembering a painful event, accepting that it happened as it did and letting go of any attachment to the pain it caused. It is not forgetting, condoning, tolerating, enabling or self-sacrificing;' It is an act of acknowledging and forgiving ourselves looking deep within. 'It's the thought of no longer carrying around the pain. It is an accepting and letting go. It's an act of self-love'[10] Rev. Ashli Callaway, MDiv and Emily Francis.

I found it helpful to think of it as putting all the pain into a bubble, bubbles like we blow for children, to blow all our pain into the bubble, then blow that bubble away. Let it be taken on the wind, let it travel far away from us until it is broken and as we are freed from it, it dissipates. Free from the pain and fear, what a lovely way for us to feel good about ourselves. Feel pity for the arsehole who will forever remain an arsehole, as they will never understand – time to let that feeling go, no need to carry it around anymore. Narcissists never understand as they think the world revolves around them.

I am still working on this forgiveness. Like everything, and like me, you might find it all takes time. It might take a few bubbles full of painful thoughts and emotions, but keep going it gets easier.

When we feel unhappy, we are not able to see the big picture due to feelings of frustration and loss of control. But when we feel happy, we are positive in our thoughts. This, in turn, provides us with the ability to keep life in perspective, feel calm and be in control. It may be difficult sometimes, but find time to have some fun, even in the smallest of moments; the child inside us with innocent eyes will come out and play. Count your blessings as it will remind you that you have much to be grateful for.

As I said previously, it is about our outlook. No one can see, take or use our thoughts. Our thoughts are our own and belong to us. Sure, we can share them, if we want to, with friends or a loved one. The more we set out to have positive thoughts, the more we can experience warm and cuddly emotions, the more we come to enjoy life. Live in the moment and enjoy each moment, and at the end of the day be grateful for these moments, no matter how small or large. The way we are in any given moment is what helps define us. Think positivity and fun. Once you get into the habit of it, it not only becomes easier but feels delightful.

Such moments do not have to involve big ticket items, they can be times when you appreciate the little things in life. One such moment for me was while living at my brother's house in Victoria. It was pouring with rain. Between the downpours a flock of galahs (an Australian cockatoo), nine of them in all, perched on the power lines out the front of the house. As I was watching them, I noticed that as each downpour of rain came, they hung upside down with their wings out, having a bath. What a fantastic thing to be privileged to see.

Sometimes it is just as healing to sit and chill, watching the events of life go by, how the birds or other animals interact with each other and with nature itself. When the storm clouds move through, sit in the warmth and watch them. When the sun comes out after the rain, everything is clean and fresh, leaves sparkle in the sun and the wildlife comes out to forage on the new growth. Nature truly is the most wonderful gift for bringing healing. We need to take notice and appreciate it. Nature nurtures us as we go through life's traumatic events. It can also assist us to reflect on our life experiences.[32] I make sure I spend time each day, even if only for a few moments, to sit and appreciate nature. If I don't, the birds come and let me know when it is time for a break. The crimson rosellas land on the flyscreen of my window and look in. It makes me laugh. It's as if they are indeed telling me – time for a break.

It is beneficial to learn to be still. I found that when I sit in nature, absorb it, listen and engage with it, a certain calmness comes over me. Remember to be kind to yourself, always be honest and sincere, happy, give everything your very best.

Learn to be creative. Succeed where you can regardless, and let go of those that are unreasonable or self-centered.

One of the things we learn once out of the traumatic experience of domestic violence is that it teaches us to slow down. We start to look at the world in a whole new light. We need to be careful with how we view ourselves, learn to treat and think of ourselves in a kind and patient way. No more guilt or thinking it's our fault. What I am talking about here is like when we walk into a lolly shop and marvel at the choices. This is what life is like, a lolly shop.

I was out with Renee, at a friend's place a while back. We had pizzas – wood fired – it was lovely and warm as the cold autumn nights approached. We had good conversations that were really enlightening. I came to realise there is kindness everywhere and some genuine people in this world. This was an unfamiliar feeling for me, as I had been isolated from people and having not experienced this sort of kindness, felt alien to me. In this surrounding with these old friends, I felt humbled. It was also interesting to know how others thought of me. They perceived me as being strong and self-assured, whereas I was conscious of how very insecure I felt, lacking in confidence and sensitive to the feeling's thoughts and actions of others.

When I explained this to them, they seemed surprised. I suppose after years of hiding the shame, of dealing with intimate partner violence (IPV), one learns to hide things well. Their company, the yummy pizzas, the warmth of conversation and their encouraging comments I shall treasure forever.

*

Why when meditating is it recommended that we concentrate on our breathing? It helps us to stay focused, to stay present, which is hard to do when our thoughts are running riot. It is about becoming still and calm through concentrating as we follow our breathe in and out of our body. We can settle and really begin to focus on the here and now. It helps us to become anchored. I have always found meditation very difficult, to just slow down and clear the mind of any thought was difficult for me, yet at other times out of the blue I find I'd been meditating without realising it, it's a wonderful experience. If you find it difficult to meditate, what I found worked for me was upon waking in the morning, before you get out of bed just lie there not thinking of anything just concentrate on breathing in and out for three to five breaths, just try to be still for a moment or two and then come back to yourself, try it. Remembering to do this each day is the necessity; however, it has certainly helped me. We all have a different way to experience meditation, you will find what you feel comfortable with.

I learnt that we become shallow breathers during period of stress or depression, or when we have insufficient sleep. This explained for me my years of being a shallow breather, of having to constantly sigh to gain more oxygen. Even now I often have to stop occasionally and concentrate on my breathing, making sure I take full breaths.

Meditation helped me realise that I was restricting myself, impeding the natural flow. This really hit home for me when I had a substantial anxiety attack. I was struggling to breathe, something I imagine might be like suffering an asthma attack. As I alluded to in chapter four, fortunately Simone was close by and acted immediately. I received the biggest hug from her and at the same time she was yelling in my ear. 'Breath, Mum, breath.' It was distressing not being able to breathe, but at the same time it was the loveliest of moments. Simone is quite strong, and her really big hug gave me such a feeling of security that, along with her encouraging words, it helped me get through. I never want to feel the helplessness that lack of breath caused ever again.

Consider the way we breathe. When we focus on our breathing, we begin to experience our life force we gain strength and confidence, really, we do. Through correct and focused breathing, the fear and pain we have been internalising be it through destructive thought patterns, toxins, or trauma (there is that word again) we will find ourselves thinking on a more positive note, our sense of self-worth and joy will increase. As Rebecca Dennis in her book *Breathe* states 'Breathing correctly increases our energy and calms our nervous system. It releases muscle tension and affects our mental state. And then there are all the medical benefits it brings us.' [28]

By taming our breathing, we strengthen our inner self and gain more confidence. The stronger we become, the more confident we become. Then when we face new, unexpected challenges, we can cope better and move through the challenges more quickly than we initially thought.

Research has shown that counsellors who show their 'patients open-hearted understanding and kindness are more effective than those who try to help through reaching into someone's subconscious to interpret feelings of stress and anxiety.'[16] I found this with my counsellors. When I explained the various issues and challenges, I was facing, and how I was becoming overwhelmed, my counsellor would provide an overview. A bit like taking a helicopter view. This helped to give me some clarity.

One crucial thing I have learnt is that a woman can get relief from stress by talking about her problem, or problems. <u>But we want to be heard, we don't need to be fixed.</u>

Through our journey we learn to become resilient. Resilience is the process of successfully adapting to difficult or challenging life experiences, especially through achieving mental, emotional, and behavioural flexibility. It is this flexibility that enables us to adjust to the external and internal demands we face.

Examples of resilience include: trying to take a positive perspective on a situation, seeing challenges as learning opportunities and focusing on the things we can control instead of dwelling on what we cannot change. 39

I was always in awe of friends, their self-confidence. After many years of coercive control, I was lost and found it took me considerable time me to gain confidence in myself. Look at the achievements you've made. As I've said previously, put even the smallest achievements together, they all add up to significant growth. Remember this is your life now. Remember that patience or tolerance comes from an ability to remain strong and resolute, not to be overwhelmed by the adverse situations that we face, the wet fish moments. 'It takes inner strength to remain firm in our resolve, don't view tolerance or patience is a sign of weakness, it's not.' 21 The Art of Happiness a Handbook for living – His Holiness The Dalai Lama and Howard C Cutler.

In our journey of learning or finding our resilience as we face the challenges that come across our path, we find ways to change our direction. It is in having an optimistic outlook, and having determination, that we can, and then strive forward.

Unlike the pessimist, having an optimistic outlook we are more likely to find ways to solve our problems. As an optimist we choose coping strategies like seeking emotional support, drawing on spiritual resources or we become more accepting of a situation that is outside of our control. The true optimist recognises the challenges and then ascertains how to work through these. By having an optimistic view of life, we tend to persevere and cope by using problem-solving tactics to manage pressures, to be more in control in face of the challenges that arise.

The optimist has the positive emotions of love, joy, and surprise, while the pessimist has the negative bias feelings of anger, sadness, and fear. To be happy, we must accept who we are, accept ourselves, warts and all. This then takes us to our reactions and how we cope with life. No one is perfect and we accept our friends in the same manner as they do us, warts and all.

One of the main traits of being an optimist is gratitude. Research has shown that if we get into the habit of being consciously thankful, over time we will feel more positive, and optimistic about life. I found my grateful book has been an inspiration for me, allowing me to look at the little things that I'm grateful for each day. People who are consistently grateful are happier and more satisfied with their lives, they even feel more physically healthy. Gratitude connects us to the natural world because one of the easiest things to feel grateful for is the beauty of nature. Therefore, gratitude is important for maintaining our happiness.

It becomes a belief that if we do the right thing each day then we are in fact creating a better tomorrow. Unless we practice and maintain that belief, we are likely to simply give up. Some of the most important lessons I have learnt were to find space between events, to wait, breathe, slow down and pause.

Rather than live in a state of never-ending activity (especially when under pressure or in an emotional state), take a break, then reassess. It's only with an optimistic view that we have a real chance of creating an amazing future, both for humanity and for ourselves.

'Optimism means taking the attitude that things will improve if we put some effort in.' it is one of the most beautiful personality traits. As an optimist we are often high achievers and recover faster from illness, suffering, anxiety, and depression. How do we become an optimist? Change our cognitive thinking pattern first, then change our harmful thoughts by thinking in new positive ways, look for the good. Thinking we have a problem, it's the thought, this is the problem itself.

How we view, and contextualise a challenge when we are in crisis, and what we tell ourselves it means, determines how difficult it will be to overcome. By having the right perspective, the right thought pattern, we can find the way to break down the challenge into little bites, then move forward with

> *Whenever you find yourself doubting how far you can go, just remember how far you have come*
>
> *Remember **everything** you have faced, all the battles you have won, and all the fears you have overcome.*
>
> *Unknown*

structured process, and a positive method. You can enjoy the feelings of achievement as you reflect on how you navigated your way through.

I was very fortunate in that I have wonderful friends sending me captions that I put into a scrapbook. It's heartwarming to read through these and they have encouraged me in moving forward. The first slogan I received was, 'Don't look back, you're not going that way!'

There are many sayings like this that have helped me no end to stay focused and keep going. It's very easy to fall back and wonder if it's all worth it. Many go back only to find themselves in a worse situation.

> '*Make the most of the best and the least of the worst*'
> Robert Louis Stevenson. 22

Love begins from within. We must first learn to acknowledge ourself and care for our inner emotions in order to gradually gain strength. What we will find over time is that love radiates from deep down, this gives us a feeling of release as it sets us free. Sometimes it may be difficult to experience this, depending on what life situations, environments and experiences we are going through at the time. We do what we can to survive, there is no love to live in fear or survival, only anxiety about finding a way to live from one day to the next day. We live in hope that life will get better, will change, but we need to help it along the way, help to make the move to break free.

I understand one of the great joys of falling in love is the feeling that the most extraordinary person in the entire world has chosen you. That is, as long as you love this person and they love you back with the same intense feeling of deep affection, of conviction, respect, and devotion.

Once we leave a violent relationship and we have gone through a journey of self-discovery, we identify what it is that we really want from life. In our journey we gain a newfound confidence in ourselves, and find new friends in addition to the treasured and reliable old friends. Friends are to be treasured and taken into our hearts; we learn a lot from our friends.

Of all the things that wisdom delivers for living a life of happiness, the greatest by far is the possession of friendship.

Moving beyond the immediate challenges of leaving a relationship that has involved intimate partner violence, and beginning to face the world afresh, peeking into the lolly shop and choosing a different lolly to try, looking for new ways to be part of the world, we could find that the old career is no longer useful, that it does not suit us anymore. It may not have been obvious at the time, especially while dealing with the emotional and financial difficulties involved in untangling a relationship, but these life changes have the potential to open the possibility for new opportunities. This journey has happened for me, after having read a number of books and gained understanding through my counsellor. I stated at the time I was seeing her that I wanted to be able to help others who go through similar traumas. We are all different and cope differently; although we may have similar experiences, we process things differently. We all go into our dark places, our rabbit holes, but these help us to learn and grow, change, and move forward. Helping each other and giving back is a rewarding emotion. Embrace it.

We are always in charge of our own mind and we can help it grow by using it the right way. Opening ourselves up to growth makes us more of ourselves, not less. If we already have self-control, then it is a matter of harnessing it in the right direction.

Some find it easy to stay in their unhappiness going over an unhappy incident again and again it becomes like a constant spiral, some become comfortable in this sadness as it is now the only thing they know. These traumas can become your identity – do not let them. It is a very hard cycle to break and work your way out of, especially if you are strong willed or proud and do not easily accept help from others. However, there will come a time when we feel the need to break free from this negative cycle and 'Have Some Fun.' Also never underestimate the power of listening to music. My granddaughter loves music and loves to dance, she showed me how to download music onto my phone, I can have it with me always. What a lovely gift to give.

I found that listening to music is one of the quickest and simplest ways to enhance my mood and energy. According to research music stimulates parts of the brain that trigger happiness; it relaxes the body. It has even been shown that during medical procedures it can lower the patients' blood pressure and anxiety levels.

There are many fantastic songs which I used each day to help me feel happy. Find the ones that make you feel good. It will depend on your mood as to what you pick, but go for it, as it really does help. I have come to pay more attention to the lyrics within each song now, I had not always noticed all of them previously. Some songs that I like are from Lobo, Russell Morris, Pink, Robbie Williams, Adele, Ed Sheeran, Lady Gaga and Joe Cocker I could go on and on; there are many great songs by great artists.

*

I keep reiterating that it's important that we appreciate the journey as much as we enjoy the outcome; reflect, and look back at how far we have come, what we have achieved, even in what we might feel, how our feelings have changed. It might sometimes be the smallest of events that can bring about these changes. We did it and we did it with the help of counsellors, friends, and family. But most importantly we found our inner strength to accomplish even the smallest of things through to the biggest.

Never forget that to prevent ourselves against falling into apathy or depression when facing difficult circumstances, we need to find our inner strength and change our outlook, our cognitive thinking, and be an optimist. [29]

Domestic violence, no matter what shape or form it takes, is tough going; there is no denying that. But in forging a way out, we can look for happier days ahead. Happiness is a state of mind, like positive thinking is a state of mind. It is a bit like giving up smoking; once you have made your mind up to stop, then it is easier to do. The hard part is making the actual decision to stop. Sticking to it and reminding ourself how much better we will feel, comes easier after that. If I can stop the habit of smoking, then anyone can.

To have an optimistic outlook, to remain positive, is critical in our efforts to move forward. Yes, we all have our own journey. Quite often I would say, 'I am damaged goods. Who would want me?' I have had to learn to accept what I have been through and to change my thinking in order to start to move ahead, gaining back my optimistic attitude. Be grateful for the small moments. Sometimes we get big moments and they knock us over, but they are moments all the same. Cherish the positives even the small ones are illuminating. Capture these moments. Be grateful. It is good to reflect as I see the journey that I have travelled.

Once we become a bit older and wiser, we realise that our happiness is derived from who we are and not what we have. Realise it's not a competition about what we do and do not possess; it is not a status symbol. But when we think like this, we have missed the point to life, well I think so anyway. All these possessions we work hard for do not necessarily bring us pleasure, and we cannot take them with us. But what we hold dear to our heart deep inside, the love, joy and surprises we share with friends and family along the way, this is happiness. It is the way they make us laugh, be it a joke or something funny we remember. If something makes us smile, gives us a warm feeling inside (like a child getting a cuddle) or makes us laugh till our sides hurt, then this is living a happy, contented life, in my eyes anyway. Sure, we all have bad experiences but each one of us has our own life experiences which takes us on a journey. It is how we progress and move forward through our journey that defines us. Stay positive, be the optimist look for the new doors to open and new opportunities. They are out there. It takes us time to find them. Some of us, like me, take longer than others to find our way in the journey, but that is okay it is what makes us different.

I was and I am still learning and growing, after a while, believe it or not, the odd occasions where life does become fun happens more frequently. It is a great feeling. I am hoping, with my journey, although I am only in the early stages, that I experience more of these fun moments. Especially the warm cuddly moments which can come in many a different form.

I keep going on about this; however, it is important that we remember it is through our mistakes, hardship and less than desirable situations that we learn. This in turn can drive us onto new and exciting adventures. It may be hard to see this when you are in a bad situation but these experiences place us on a road to recovery where we then learn to fly, so to speak, and along the way we have reconnected and/or met new people that might not otherwise have crossed our path. However again it must all be done in <u>little bites</u>.

Clean out the debris from within on a regular basis. What do we really want to carry around with us and what can we discard? It is important to ask ourselves, 'Why do I need to hang onto this thought or memory, what purpose does it serve me?' I found a good clean out does improve feelings of well-being. Sure, sometimes thoughts sneak back in, but the second or third time around it is not as difficult to clean them out.

Pretending to be happy when you are in pain, is an example of how strong you are as a person. However, you are not being true to yourself by pretending. Stay focused and acknowledge yourself, know your worth, your strong because of what you have been through. This is where you gained your strength. Look at how far you have come.

<u>Never underestimate the healing power of touch</u>, then breathe. We are enough just as we are. Look at the world as through innocent eyes, it is amazing. It's in overcoming fear that courage lives.

CHAPTER TEN

EYES TO THE SOUL

As William Shakespeare quoted, 'Our eyes are the window to our soul.' Unfortunately, many of us must fall apart before we find new ways of beginning again. When we let go of what has been trapping us, we can begin to feel compassion and love. No longer do we think, 'I'm not good enough.' We change our thinking and perspective, not only feeling our inner strength grow, but we become enthused and passionate about what we need to do to gain the confidence to be able to achieve whatever we want. Instead of running around like a chook with its head cut off we slow down, look within, find the peace within yourself before moving forward. This was what my counsellor kept trying to tell me – I was to slow down, give myself a break and take little bites.

As I have said in a previous chapter, some of the morals my mum had taught me when I was young were independence and self-control—very useful traits to have. The other most important thing Mum taught me was to keep an open mind. This, she instilled in me, when she had finished the studies she had undertaken on all the various religions.

Growing up in primary school, our Sunday mornings were spent attending Sunday School followed by going to church, followed by a lovely roast for lunch. It was not until much later, that I discovered Mum had been taking the sermons to all the people who wanted to go to church but could not physically get there. She would read the sermon to them and then return it to the vicar. However, after a while, Mum grew a bit despondent with the teachings of the church and set out to read everything she could lay her hands on about all the various religions. She would then impart this knowledge to us as children. I could not help but soak this all up. Move over Lobsang Rampa, Mum had more interesting information. From all her learnings, though, the motto, 'Keep an open mind' is one I have kept to this day – receive what you see, read and hear into yourself, digest it, take what you want from it, not what you think you need or others feel you must take on board.

Once we place our attention on giving, having no desire to get anything in return, we experience peace of mind and a sense of inner peace and joy. Ask yourself do you want to experience Love or Fear? Do you choose to look for the positives in all things or to find fault in all things?

I found we need to continually remain motivated. Success and fulfillment rests in our ability to get up each day, willing ourselves to the next level, to the next goal. Sure, we do not always know what that goal is. Most of us automatically think that it should be a big goal, something that is a standout. As I mentioned previously, it does not have to be a big goal, getting up and going for a walk is a goal, that is a standout. Take in all your surroundings as you walk, be it along the road or along the beach or in a park, take notice of the wildlife around you. The birds get up each day and forage for their meal to feed their young and themselves. Isn't that what we do? We feel motivated because we choose to, it is an energy that results from thought.

We set ourselves some goals. Start with little bites and work them into our new life. Take time to make clearer choices and more deeply commit to the goals, to energise ourselves and pursue these goals. Do not stop at one. Once we achieve one goal, before reaching the outcome and celebrating the achievement, start to think about what the next goal might be, what we would like to do. What is stopping us? Only our own fears. When we change our attitude, we begin to heal.

*

As I discussed in chapter nine, once I had started to move on in my recovery from the domestic violence I experienced, I could begin looking at where I might want to go career-wise. Except for the position I took up when I had not really given myself enough time to recover fully from domestic violence, I now realise it was too much too soon. In the past, I would go in slowly when starting in a new role in my working career. I would take in the surroundings, the environment and personalities of staff and management, getting the lay of the land. Anyone can make a change to a business, but are they making changes for the sake of it (to put their own mark on the business = ego) or are they making the business more productive, more functional, not only for the clients they serve but also for the staff? Having this awareness was a useful tool for me on my own journey to find myself and for dealing with the situations I was experiencing in life once I was out. All too often, we become a slave to our egos. During my working career, I was always very conscious of not letting the ego control my actions; the need now is to be authentic to the real me, for me.

What have we learnt from this? – I hope not only to inspire ourselves, but also to inspire others on our journey, be that in our working life, socialising or life in general. It feels good to let ourselves be free of tension and conflict, because at the end of the day, how much is our ego really worth? When we really analyse this, Ego equates to Fear.

No one can take our thoughts away from us (I keep saying this, as it is important to acknowledge). Sure, they can influence us, but in the end, when we peek past the cloud, then the thought and choice is ours for the taking. By dwelling on negative thoughts and past injuries, whether they are emotional or physical, the beautiful person inside us does not grow and we stifle ourselves. LET GO. Take that step. I know it is easier said than done but, believe me, once we have stepped out beyond the cloud, once we have escaped and taken our time to find ourself, life is like a lolly shop.

Which lolly will you choose today? I like the Choo Choo bar, but maybe you would prefer the Polly Waffle?

On my journey I have had to learn patience although it still is quite a challenge. I have had jobs where I had responsibilities that required me to think on my feet as I went through risk assessments in my head; I had to move the businesses forward continually, acting in the best interest of others, with responsibility for many businesses, clients and staff. I found this came easily to me. However, learning to be patient with myself has been an extremely hard slog, though a very rewarding one. The more I practice patience, the better I am.

I have always loved the various gems and stones and what they can bring to my life. I think it is important for us to use whatever we feel comfortable with to help us through, I brought myself a bracelet of howlite. Howlite is most commonly thought of as a stone for patience and calm and is known for helping us to slow down. It is also considered to be particularly helpful for moving through deep emotions and unrest. I would like to think that my bracelet has helped me, and anything that has helped me has been a bonus. It is all a matter of perspective, I suppose.

Acceptance of change on any level allows life to flow, bringing new joys we might not otherwise have imagined. Nothing remains the same; no one day is the same as the previous one, and when life throws change our way, trying to resist or control only leads to more suffering.

There will be plenty of wet fish moments, but if you think about it, what are these moments telling us? What can we learn from them? Through personal experience, I learnt that it comes down to how we choose to react to these challenging events. When we find ourselves in the midst of dealing with challenging events, we need to remember to rest, experience our feelings and allow these feelings to work their way out. Reflecting on our decisions before moving forward again in who knows what direction, can be half the fun, finding the way we are going to travel. Scary? Absolutely, but if we grab the opportunity before us with both hands and an open-heart, we can think of the exciting journey it might take us on.

True love conquers all, and that can apply to what we do and experience in life or who we love in life.

It is hard but true and we need to learn to acknowledge and love ourselves first before we can love others. Not *thinking* we love but actually *loving* someone that leaves you breathless, (Remember to breathe though). Nature has much to teach if we are only open to the learning.

Through all of our life's challenges and learnings, in the end it is still up to us as to what we choose to focus on; we are free to follow our own rite of passage. Until my escape, I had allowed the opinions of others to guide and shape me rather than claim my own entitlement to happiness. However, as I've said, I am an optimist and prefer to keep an open mind. I have learnt from my mistakes and changed my goals where needed, always aiming to choose happiness. We are all worthy of happiness, are we not?

The choices we make in life become lessons for our souls. Trust is the greatest emotion, and with trust we gain faith and attract happiness. I'd like to expand on the meanings of Trust here again, expanding on what was covered in chapter six.

Trust is the bedrock of every solid meaningful relationship, even the relationship with yourself.

One extremely difficult task is to forgive yourself, we all have different feelings, emotions, personalities. I had to forgive myself for being so insecure, for not leaving earlier, for living in fear and not moving out sooner, for not being a better care giver to my children. I could go on but you get my drift. In the end, I realised that my insecurity was part of me, all the personal traits I had were the ones that made me who I was and am. This is an extremely confronting emotion to work through; in the end you find yourself, you accept and forgive yourself. Own it and be proud of yourself. Trusting yourself, is important in order to progress in life.

Without trust, love is vulnerable and weak. Build that trust and you stand invincible either alone or more importantly with a partner.

Claiming to love someone and at the same time saying you don't trust them is a misguided kind of love; you will always be wondering and second guessing, and the toxic burden will eat away your soul, eventually bringing about collapse of the relationship.

So, is trust the foundation of love? Absolutely! Can love for another exist without trust? Maybe for a while, but it is destined to shatter.

Along life's journey we not only learn about life in general but more importantly about ourselves. Sometimes this is a very tough journey and confronting but it can be a wonderful experience which depends on our attitude and feelings. Through self-acknowledgement we continue to learn and grow.

We can gain our freedom through physical and emotional stages. We can acknowledge ourselves and be kind to ourselves, as well as others. Always be respectful of the feelings of others. Stop and think, 'Would I like to be treated this way?' If the answer is no, then do not pursue it. If you are being honest and truthful, passionate and kind, these are the most important qualities within us that we can carry throughout life's journey. Our main task in life is to enjoy it, no judgement or justification, be the glorious person we were meant to be. It is giving ourselves permission to shine. All our dreams are waiting for us, and when we can smile and say with courage and vulnerability, 'Yes', a whole new journey begins.

After a while, we come to realise that we do not need the old version of ourselves anymore. We have grown out of that old skin and we have in front of us the prospect of a new fun-loving and exciting self. We can go with the flow and enjoy all the happiness we deserve. Remember, it's about taking little bites. We should not overexert ourselves, as we have come through a lot. Instead, acknowledge what we have achieved, and do this often. It will help us grow in confidence to continue and move forward. Every day is a new day. Discard all those old negative thoughts and move forward. Welcome the day with open arms, enjoy each moment no matter what it is. By placing our trust in the universe, we can reach for a life full of delight.

Like me, you might find helpful books on your path fall into your hands, one flowing on from the other. In the end, what you come to realise is the truth is the truth, and you can find your own healing path. It is not an easy journey but be persistent, feel free to find yourself and let go of all the pain from the past, it is not helping you. Now is the time to welcome the new version of ourselves, make the choices that feel right for us—loving choices. Live the life our heart wants; it is okay to be you, be grateful for our freedom of choice. Take that one little bite, just one bite, initially, then take the next little bite. Rest assured it does get easier.

Let go of anything that is not genuine and any activities that do not reflect your goals for yourself. If something is not working in your life, be willing to release it, let it go. Place it in that bubble and blow it away with love. Once we decide to be true to ourselves, miracles come our way, and when they do, you will be in awe. I certainly was.

Through this journey I have been reminded across various sources, mainly those that I have read, to view the world with open eyes, to capture my sense of wonder. I am a bit slow at times and it can take a while for things to digest. This has been a good thing, as along the way it has taught me patience, endurance and tolerance towards myself. I have always been persistent, that trait wasn't hard to nurture. It was reflection, complete appreciation, gratitude, indebtedness, thankfulness and true acknowledgement I had to learn to embrace—foremost for myself, as well as others. With innocent eyes, I moved forward, and you can also. Life ahead is yet to be explored and savoured.

If we let go of any hesitation or fears we have of exposing our inner self (easy to say, hard to practise and develop as a habit), what we often find is astounding. I am often amazed by what life brings my way. Open your innocent eyes and enjoy the journey.

With each step I took moving forward, I sought a rough outline of what I could achieve, but never knew what was around the corner. Circumstances might change along the way; I needed to be flexible enough to go with the flow and go wherever life took me. I would plan the goals to attain in three-month intervals. For example: finalise the property and assets, then have a holiday with friends, followed by having the operation on my knee. Next, get a divorce and then find a property to purchase. I chose to stay positive, forever the optimist, although it did become exhausting at times. I kept persevering, whatever and wherever the journey was taking me, despite the challenges I had to face along the way.

As recent events have continued to reveal there are many women who have been through similar or worse domestic violence experiences. Look at the statistics in Australia alone:
- 1 in 6 women have experienced physical or sexual violence by a current or former partner, while for men it is 1 in 16.

- 75 per cent of victims of domestic violence reported the perpetrator as male, while 25 per cent reported the perpetrator as female.
- Overall, 1 in 5 women and 1 in 20 men have experienced sexual violence.
- On average, 1 woman every 9 days and 1 man every month is killed by a current or former partner [27]

But let us not get carried away with ourselves as not all men are tarred with the same brush. I have met some amazing men who care deeply for their partners. It is the most beautiful sight to see. It brings considerable warmth to see two people very much in love and supportive of each other. The narcissists, on the other hand, will never experience true love as their love is focused on themselves—their egos rule.

One important aspect to consider as we grow is not to try and reinvent ourselves. Get to know the hidden parts of yourself first, there is no need to be someone you're not, be yourself and learn to accept yourself as you are, after all you are a beautiful person and you are growing stronger each day. Be your own true self, you've been through a lot and you've gained your strength, know your worth and value the moments. Remember solitude is not a weakness, but a testament to your strength.

I recently had an old school friend advise me not to rush into another relationship. I think he was speaking from his own experience, though I am not sure. But, on reflection, I believe everyone is different and every individual will know when they are ready for commitment.

It is an interesting journey we are all on.

PART THREE

Take time out. Be silent and sit quietly in nature. Open up and feel free. We all want to live our lives to the fullest. We are capable, every minute, and all we need to do is show up.

CHAPTER ELEVEN

WEDDING CELEBRATIONS

Over the years my son Kai had tested me to the extreme. There were occasions I didn't laugh, like the times I would receive a phone call from Kai letting me know he was in hospital for one reason or another. The last one, he was overseas on a skiing holiday when he had a broken collarbone, a fall while snowboarding in Japan. 'But I'm okay, Mum,' he told me. It's only after the fact that we tend to talk about it and have a little laugh or smile.

Although I felt I was getting stronger, and slowly gaining some self-confidence within myself the emotions of possible confrontations brought home the fact that I was still extremely fragile. It does not matter how prepared I felt I was, there were times of panic and anxiety; after living in domestic violence for 40 years, it takes time to mend. As a mother, my children are the most important part of my life. The marriage of my youngest was the one event I was not going to miss attending, no matter what.

*

There was absolute excitement in the air with the news of my youngest son Kai's engagement. Everyone was invited to the engagement party. And unbeknown to everyone except only family the wedding ceremony was actually going to take place immediately before the 'engagement' party started. It did not turn out to be a secret though, as a few of Kai's mates pressured him for a date that they planned to marry, and Kai spilled the beans a few days prior to the engagement party, everyone was invited to the wedding ceremony too. Excitement was in the air.

But I needed a safety plan: to prepare myself for any contact with Him. Also, it was important to journal when I felt good, to acknowledge how far I had come. The brain scrambles and explodes when you are going through another potentially distressing event. As the time drew closer, I felt panicked that I was losing my train of thought and was letting the emotions of fear take over. I needed to settle, to refocus. It had not even been 12 months since I escaped, and feelings were raw.

A plan needed to be put into place, and that plan was that if at any time I felt stressed or anxious I was to phone or text my counsellor. I was not going to let anyone stop me from attending; this was my baby's wedding and I was not going to miss it for anything.

In the end I had asked Kai if he could ask Him not to approach me or talk to me on the day. Apparently, when Kai asked Him, He spat the dummy and refused to attend, I was told. I was supported by Kai and Natt, my future daughter in law, I will be forever grateful to them both.

The night before the big day arrived. I was disappointed when I discovered James and Simone weren't taking Kai out for a drink on the day before his wedding to celebrate. After all, James was in the bridal party, and being a brother, I had thought he would organise something. I felt Kai was also disappointed, I caught up with Kai and his best man, Jaden. The three of us had a great time it was great fun. We tried the different types and ages of scotch, tasting them in shot glasses, and Jaden had organised for all Kai's mates to go out for dinner together that night, a boys' night out. Although I was invited, I explained to them, 'no no this is a boy's night. Who wants to have your mum go along. Go out and have fun.'

Having those scotches together, the three of us, was the most enjoyable time. I left them to it, giving them enough time to prepare for their boys' night out! Knowing these two boys, it would have been wild yet, a really fun time for them.

During this time, I was regularly reminded by my counsellor to 'Take small steps.' I was constantly challenging myself and moving forward but I needed to do more for me for now. I felt very vulnerable and challenges gripped me. I was advised that if I was not comfortable with someone's conversation, I was to ask the question, 'what do you mean by that?' My thoughts were constantly racing. I needed to give myself time to build trust, self-confidence and feel safe.

I was starting to honour myself and gradually gaining self-acceptance, I was stepping on through. I needed to remember to breathe and to take those little bites, as I really wanted to enjoy Kai and Natt's wedding. My mind was continually racing through, with thoughts going in all directions. I needed to pause and breathe.

Over the previous few weeks, I had been thinking what I wanted to say to Kai and Natt. Once I was finally happy with what I had put together, I wrote it out on some beautiful writing paper that Simone had given me as a gift from her recent trip around Italy. Came the day, I wrote down a speech for the wedding and another letter to Kai, something for him to keep.

I was an absolute mess on the day. I thought I saw His car drive past the place I was staying. I had been texting Renee and sending photos of my accommodation, and seeing His car - or thinking I'd seen it - made me panic. I phoned Renee.

Renee was very helpful. She distracted my thoughts; with a really long chat about the antics, we go up to at school. She started to talk about the first film we made together, which was on a school camp. It was fun making that film. Renee had written the script and recruited fellow students to become involved. I oversaw the camera and filmmaking. Over the phone, we reminisced for ages about the fun, the laughter and the incidents that had taken place. I remembered how the film had been shown in the school hall, with photos and stories told of our school vacation adventure. Such great memories.

It was good to laugh and to have the distraction. By the end of the phone call, I felt more relaxed, more comfortable, and able to cope with the day ahead, no matter what came my way. I am grateful to Renee for helping me through this.

When it was nearing time for the ceremony, James and wife, along with Simone and husband arrived. After some time, James walked over to me and said hi, then he turned his back to me.

I do not need to tell you how that made me feel, but he and his wife will have to live with themselves and their actions. I am growing stronger within myself now. Besides, this was Kai's Day, not theirs, nor mine. Their problem, not mine. (I can say that now, but at the time the intention to hurt me was there, and they succeeded). Simone, on the other hand, did stand beside me and say hello, but we could not get past that. One day we will. Everything was still very raw for us all of us.

It was a beautiful wedding, held in the park near the marina on the Sunshine Coast. At the reception in the yacht club, it came my time to give a speech. I was glad I had written it down; it made it easier. However, I did take a few deep breaths to calm myself before speaking. It was short and sweet, and at the completion I folded it up and placed it in an envelope and gave it to Kai and Natt. I was flabbergasted at the response I received, not only from Kai and Natt, but from many of their other friends, mates and relatives. They commented that my speech was lovely, that I was strong to be able to stand up there and deliver the speech. They all appreciated it and loved it. I was relieved. And happy for Kai and Natt, and grateful it was well received.

I left a little later, still a bit shaken from all the emotions I was going through; I drove back to the apartment. As I drove into the tiny downstair car park I was concentrating intently on not hitting the car beside me that I scrapped my car against the pillar. I promptly backed up, drove down and then reversed into the car space; I feel more comfortable reversing. It was a breeze. I'd worry about the damage tomorrow. It was my new work car. Well, I was off to a great start with the job; 'Oh by the way I damaged the car. What paperwork do you require me to complete?' Hmmm!

Another change, another challenge, life is about to change, I'm optimistic, there is something to learn from this, I move forward believing something wonderful is about to happen. I need to live in the moment, in this minute and absorb and take in the changes.

CHAPTER TWELVE

MOVING FORWARD

It's important that we don't wait for permission or, as I found, wait for perfect timing. We must be courageous and self-reliant, find that inner strength to move forward at a moment's notice.

Love is in our nature and the most abundant resource in the universe. Love created and lives in all things. What we need to do now it is important to allow love back into our lives, and learn to love ourselves before we can direct it towards others. Easier said than done for most of us, but it is achievable over time. Everything we require to begin this great journey towards a free and fulfilled life is already within us.

Some of us learn that in life it doesn't matter what happens to us, well it does, and it matters what we do with what happens, and what we've been given to work with to move forward.

We can be spirited on by our failures and challenges while learning to smile again through the process. With each failure or challenge, the world is trying to tell us something, helping us to grow and improve. Then to be able to turn our disappointments and upsets into opportunities. Failure shows us the way by showing us what **isn't** the way. We learn to develop a process, one movement after another, little bites. One distraction or lapse into confusion can most certainly lead to setbacks. I found the key for me was to 'Stop and pause for a moment, take a breath and revitalise myself through deep breathing. Break it down (into little bites) and smile.' We learn over time to take our time, not to rush, as some problems are harder than others. By breaking it down, we can deal with the difficulties right in front of us first, then come back to others later. We all get there through taking little bites.

It takes learning one's own strength, recognising that we can take a stand, to overcome the obstacles. Sometimes it's not by attacking the obstacles but by withdrawing. We can use the actions of others against themselves instead of against us. What matters is whether a certain approach gets you to where you want to go. Using obstacles against themselves is very different from doing nothing. Only you will know what approach works in the various situations that come to you, trust yourself. Obstacles are all sent as a test, some might be viewed as minor, but in truth they are all significant.

As mentioned in previous chapter, it was a few months after the wedding that I began my journey driving from Queensland to Victoria, over 2100 kilometres drive while suffering from Covid 19.

Renee asked if I could take photos of my travels but unfortunately the route that I took did not have many safe places to stop for photos.

I sent this email instead as I reflected on my journey down between the states.

Hi Renee,

Well as I have said throughout, this has been an interesting journey.

I cannot thank you enough for the effort you went to in getting everyone together whilst I was down in Feb/March and I really loved the time we had together; it was fun thank you.

I think I mentioned that I don't make promises as promises are only made to be broken, however, I value my word and if I give my word then I live by it unless something unforeseen in life happens. I gave you my word that our friendship counts and I sincerely mean that and thank you for your support and friendship and your ongoing words of encouragement and best wishes, they are of tremendous help and support to me.

It's 2am and if I don't write this down then it would play on my mind. I cannot sleep but I wanted to share this experience with you.

Between the GPS in the car and Google maps on the phone it has taken me along roads most obviously less travelled by many people. The one that comes to mind was a name of a road that I travelled on today, and you'll love this, 'Hen and Chicken Lane.' This road turned into a dirt road after the first 80 metres and was washed out in more than a few places. I began to wonder as I came across some of the local farmers driving in the opposite direction the meaning of the road. I felt like I was either playing hen or chicken as my need to stay on the road became apparent when some of them flew around the corners on the wrong side of the road. Needless to say, I played chicken most of the time!

I came to one intersection where the car GPS said to turn right and the phone maps said to turn left, thank God they still have road signs as I went straight ahead (Goulbourn).

I have travelled up and down and across the mountain ranges many times on this trip, sometimes wondering if I would find my way back to civilisation – a town would have been great – however, through all the hairpin bends up and down the mountain ranges I saw some magnificent views of the countryside. For this, I am forever grateful as throughout this trip I have witnessed the most magnificent valleys as far as the eye can see across to the ranges. They were all very different yet glorious in their own way, although I only caught glimpses, and nearly ran off the road a few times. The few heart stopping moments gave me enough of a fright to refocus and concentrate.

This drive has provided me time to reflect. Although it was very nice and I must admit ego-boosting to have school friends acknowledge different things they liked about me, it also made me realise that they only saw the surface. By this I mean when people look at you Renee, they see you are accomplished in the field that you were always meant to be in. Everyone could see what they were as individuals and their respective futures and achievements, which was a beautiful thing in itself. School forms us in that manner, I think.

However, it occurred to me that no one saw past the reflection of me, this I looked for and found on my journey, I'd been told by my first counsellor and the psychologist that I have too much empathy. Perhaps they were right, I have only ever wanted to care for and support others. Some have taken advantage of this, some haven't. This may have led to my downfall a few times, but I have always said, 'Where there is life there is hope'.

Whilst I saw the beautiful views of valleys and mountains, this was perhaps the comparison I was drawing of my life.

People only see the surface, they don't look into the valleys, the towns, the makings of an individual. I passed through a beautiful little town today in one of these valleys. It had three churches, one of stone, another where the stone had been rendered and painted over the years and another yet again which was timber with only one pub!!! Bit of a reversal of the usual Aussie towns. You could feel the embodiment of this town and the people in it, warm and inviting with a strong backbone.

Tomorrow, I continue my journey. I feel the worst of the Covid is over (please don't let that be my famous last words), catching Covid and driving all this distance is not the best way to travel. At least I was isolated. I have managed to eat some food after the gastro so perhaps that is what is giving my body some of its strength back.

I'm now weary, however, happy to have written this down for you, perhaps. I haven't been able to take pictures of the scenery and send to you as promised. But please know this certainly is the most magnificent country, much to see.

As I head further south the colours of Autumn greet me. It's good to see autumn colours, something you don't get much of in Queensland.

Well as you can read, a bit too much for a phone text.

Hope you have a wonderful day, take care, big hugs.

Bobbin

*

Nature, in all its majestic beauty and complexity holds profound lessons for us, we need to pay attention, observe, listen. Once we digest this, nature shows us how to be resilient, the importance of grounding, and about the strength of quiet reflection.

Like a mountain we all possess an inherent strength and stability, we utilise this in our everyday life even though we are not always aware of this. It's through meditation we explore the resilience that resides within us. I found when I was thrown to the floor, nature stepped in. I was shaken and felt my core revealed itself to me. It's occurrences like this that invite us to find ourselves, to find our inner strength, and to stand tall, and unshaken regardless of the conditions around us. Initially I found meditation difficult, it was because I was trying too hard. Once I relaxed, and went with the flow it became easier each time.

As I travelled through the mountains and valleys I was encouraged to pause and reflect, it's not only the mountains we encountered in life, not the physical mountains but the metaphorical ones.

When we think about the times, we've felt our resilience tested, the moments we've had to stand firm in the face of adversity. These experiences, become part of our character, shaping us into peaceful yet strong individuals we are today.
Each breath moves us towards inner peace, each moment of awareness is a reinforcement of our resilience. By allowing ourselves to be inspired by the mountain's unwavering presence; it teaches us about standing firm, whist the valleys show us how to appreciate the power and beauty of our inner strength.

This unwavering core lies within each of us, a core of strength and serenity. It providing us with the ability to withstand adversity, one that remains steadfast through the storms of life. As we move forward in our journey.

CHAPTER THIRTEEN

REFLECTION

I passed my hardest moments alone, while everyone believed I was fine.

One constant that I found was a pain in the arse was having to consistently update my address, which was a necessity. There was updating the vehicle registration, power bill, or any utility or personal information. At the outset, I found I got used to explaining to the person on the phone that I was a DV victim/survivor. This was to ensure that they do not impart any of my personal information to old email addresses, or in the instances where some records in the past had both names. For some service providers this does not compute, I had one such incident when I went to obtain home insurance. I first questioned them to ensure they had the correct email address. No, they still had the old one. I explained to them I did not want the old email address used as I no longer had access to it, only He did, then I gave them my new email address. They confirmed via my new email that they had updated my details. What they also did was send notification to my old email address. I then had to explain the implications of this to the service person, as I did not want any of my details relating to the address or my purchase of a home to Him. She assured me this would not happen. It is like an ongoing saga having to ensure all my personal details remain personal for my own protection. In all instances it caused angst and is not helpful as regards your emotions; it plays havoc.

Sometimes it builds up and you start to feel like you're drifting down the spiral again. This is when it pays to talk to a counsellor or a good friend. In my case I phoned a good friend. It was more to vent and have a sook, as I'd had a few wet fish moments that week in addition to the above.

While going for a stress test I accidentally knocked the stop button with my elbow, I had to commence all over again. I had explained to the hospital staff my concerns regarding recovering from my knee operation. Nonetheless we started again. When we were more than half way through the second time, my legs gave way and I collapsed, sliding into the desk behind the machine and bending both knees right back. I had to get help to stand up, off to emergency I go. To cut a long story short plenty of ice and stay off the knee for a few days till I have a follow-up appointment with my GP.

Accepting help along with compliments from people is not only a strange feeling, but also sometimes very hard to get used to. Well, this has always been the case for me. It does take time to process and get used to the new feelings that come over me. For such an extensive period I felt unworthy. Care and kindness expressed by other people was a difficult emotion to learn to accept. It's easier to give to others than to accept the same kindness in return; it pulls at my heartstrings. I am grateful to many people, be it friends or acquaintances.

Coming out of DV, there are experiences that we find strange, often difficult to encounter again however illuminating. The feelings and renewed experiences we have involve: - being able to go shopping on our own; purchasing foods that we like; playing the music we enjoy listening to as it brings renewed hope as we lose ourselves in the music and lyrics; actually wearing clothing that makes us feel good, which helps us in our journey to gain our confidence back; coming away from the hairdressers feeling comfortable knowing that we are not going to encounter any denigration once home. These seemingly small errands might appear insignificant to those who have not experienced domestic violence, however for those of us who have, these are enormous hurdles.

The non-lethal strangulation He committed against me was not the only incident where He was violent like this. While we were managing a tourist resort park in New South Wales, there was an occasion where He had a run in with a patron from the park; she was drunk, but that's no excuse. We were living upstairs above the office, storage, and meeting rooms. She had come around late at night, standing outside the building, and banging on the glass windows of the office downstairs. He went downstairs to see what all the ruckus was about. After a short time, I could hear them both arguing and fighting, I went downstairs to investigate. I opened the door to the outside paved area; he had her back bent over the railing and his hands around her neck trying to strangle her. I yelled at them both.

He wanted her to know he could take her life so easily, that she meant nothing.

Memories came flooding back, a push a shove or a fist coming at me only centimetres from my face making a hole in the door just beside my head. The terror instilled in me came to the fore; I froze as all the memories came rushing back. I felt for her yet at the time couldn't help, I was too scarred, my feet frozen to the ground.

He went inside, and then she approached me. Holding my hands up, I asked her not to touch me. Moving towards me, the look we shared as our eyes met, was a mirror reflection - she recognised the same fear, I felt so sorry I couldn't console her. All I could do was watch as, she turned around and went back to her van.

Once upstairs he noticed she had dug her nails into his arm and drawn blood, as you would if someone was trying to strangle you. You try to get their hands off you any way you can. He threatened me, making it abundantly clear what I could and could not say to the police or else. Then he phoned the police. He was more concerned with the police locking her up for the night than admitting what he had done to her. Now ask yourself, does being drunk and abusive warrant being strangled?

It is of no consequence how long ago the strangulation happened to me; it remains with you as if it only happened yesterday. Ask anyone who has been through it. I ask, **what** justification is there for throwing a person to the floor, then attempting to strangle them, attempting to take their life? How can anyone condone this? Let us call it for what it is – strangulation, both manual and by ligature, is the most common cause of homicidal asphyxiation.

We do not get over this kind of trauma; we only learn to cope and in our own way, manage our fears, to come to terms with the traumatic experiences and move forward. It is a matter of attitude. We change the cognitive thinking. There is life after a traumatic event such as non-lethal strangulation and DV, however, as I have found, it is not only supportive but crucial in anyone's recovery to seek and receive the help of counsellors from domestic violence services who support you as you navigate your way out.

Non-fatal strangulation is used as a tactic to control victims' behaviours by:
- showing them how easily their life could be taken
- as a form of degrading and shaming them
- as a sexual act;
- to silence them

Fortunately, due to the increased awareness within society today of domestic violence, the risks and dangers associated with non-fatal strangulation have visibly improved since 2015 when the issue was highlighted by the Not Now, Not Ever Report. 31

It feels like we have been pulling teeth, but at last, things are beginning to improve, thanks to research: via coronial findings, health professionals, police and research completed and published by Jess Hill, (thank you) along with training. There is now greater awareness of the behaviour and its relationship to the broader context of IPV (intimate partner violence) and coercive control. 31

But there is a long way to go.

It is not solely the police but also magistrates who require further training and understanding to identify coercive control within the relationship, to better understand the obstacles faced in relation to the survivor's help-seeking and how they might improve the safety response.

I felt disheartened when I went to one of the local police stations to give them updates about where I was living and why. The response is still the standard 'Phone 000'. While I realise how stretched the police are, not many have learnt from the training they have received. As far as I've been able to ascertain, there has been no real funding to provide more police to support those encountering domestic violence however, I'm happy to stand corrected.

Estimates published by WHO (World Health Organisation) indicate that globally about 1 in 3 (30%) of women worldwide have been subjected to either physical and/or sexual intimate partner violence or non-partner sexual violence in their lifetime. Most of this violence is intimate partner violence. 36

Australian Bureau of Statistics data (15 March 2023) shows that 2 in 5 Australians have experienced physical or sexual violence. 36

A truly oppressive person cannot see beyond his or her own self-interest and relationships with them will never be happy. They live in a world for themselves, they are blinded by their own self-importance. Don't try to calm them and don't grovel. Abandon any hope that they can or will change. At all cost avoid letting them aggravate you. At no time sink to their level. If there is one thing I've learnt from this journey, it's to never endure a bully's efforts to control us, to restrict us or hold us back. The need is to be determined in our pursuit, to give a wide berth to these people without ever leaving or being distracted from our own journey.

In going through trauma and trying to understand and manage, the lessons I learnt were to look inward for my answer, focusing on a few important things at a time, not everything at once. It wasn't about trying to reinvent myself, rather, it was crucial that I got to know the hidden parts of me, the parts that were already there waiting for me to discover them again. There I found the child within who never grows old. I smile as I evolve.

Fear is the most powerful torture of all. You'll see women called out, judged, and burned by mainstream and social media. Know that the fear some of us feel about sharing our story, our truths and our vulnerabilities is not made up, a matter of perception or merely historical. **It's Real.**

Everyone needs to be seen AND heard, and for many of us, including me, that does not come easily. The fear that it's 'not safe' for us to speak or write or share our story, can keep us mute, and renders us powerless, with feelings of complete uselessness.

It's time to tell our story / my story. Not the voice of the 'good girl' who says what she thinks others want her to say. When I had a fierce self-belief, none could blame, shame, or make me feel 'less than.' Not someone else's truth, your truth, My Truth.

Our tomorrows are created through our thoughts, actions and words. I needed to be real and not let negative people rule my life or influence my choices. Hard learnings for me were to begin to value myself, share my light, and when another wrinkle appeared, well I needed to chalk that up to experience and reflect on all the great laughs I'm now enjoying. Although I still really struggle with this, as He always made an issue out of it, my thoughts turn to positive experiences that I now enjoy with new and old friends.

We might feel we will never smile again, but do not give up, as our smiles and laughter will and do come back and it feels great. If we watch a funny TV program or read a funny book, something might catch us by surprise and we will really laugh out loud. This is healthy and restorative for our mind, body, heart, and soul. Laugh, smile, and laugh some more. We are allowed to be happy; we deserve to be happy, and now is the time.

As I seek closure after the past 18 or more months since my escape, I reflect on what I have experienced and achieved since, only the big-ticket items:

- I escaped and I found safety and support from family, friends, and the Red Rose Foundation Queensland.
- I gained the strength to be able to go out for walks, go down the street, to the library, to the shops, unescorted and not controlled, to become familiar with the world at large – the lolly shop.
- I had many challenges come my way which really tested me but I faced them and made it through, becoming stronger.
- I went down a rabbit hole only to find myself there.
- Property and assets were finalised through the courts, and although I settled for less than half, I was relieved to be out of the relationship, to feel safe and to start my new journey in life.
- I had a wonderful holiday, caught up with many old school friends and was taken back to my roots.
- Throughout my journey I have been fortunate to have such wonderful friends and to meet many caring people.
- I applied for a divorce and the courts approved it. For me, this was closure, finalisation, the end of being the victim of having someone else with the power to manipulate, injure and control me.

- I have had a successful operation on my knee and after some rehab and physio I can now walk comfortably, and am improving all the time.
- I have been fortunate in having accommodation at my brothers' place, which provided solitude and allowed me time to compile this book.
- I hope this book in some way helps others to traverse DV. As I said at the very beginning if I have helped one person to move forward and out of domestic violence into a safer life then writing this book has been worthwhile.
- I have purchased the cutest little cottage by the ocean, which has provided me with more new projects to continue with and a new community to become involved with, volunteering comes to mind.
- With the support of friends, I developed my scrap book containing captions and quotes that helped me through.

Now is the beginning of a new journey, a new adventure. I have a few ideas of what I would like to do, however I shall be patient and optimistic, and watch to see what comes my way, not rushing but taking 'little bites.' Not only do I feel stronger but perhaps more resilient, albeit extremely vulnerable at the same time. I think this is an encouraging thing to say, as the journey still continues on.

Sometimes we relapse and this can come at the most unexpected moments. Some time ago a friend, Lee, asked me to join him for a coffee. I was not well at the time, and I gave Lee an out. He still wanted to catch up for coffee though. I was really pleased and looking forward to talking face to face, to having a conversation.

I was not prepared for what was to come, as a calm came over me.

When we met, Lee only glanced at me, before looking away. From there, while enjoying a coffee, his gaze no longer acknowledged I sat in front of him. Any engagement or real conversation ceased to exist. Preoccupied with his phone, Lee appeared more comfortable looking for accommodation for me for the night, as I was not familiar with the area and was ill. I found it disconcerting that he had asked me for coffee yet didn't see me.

The calm that came over me was a relief of sorts. We had our coffee and then he drove me to the accommodation, before we'd part ways and he went back to work.

The next day I continued my travels, and felt myself sliding backwards. I doubt Lee had any idea of the impact his ignoring me had on my self-worth.

My counsellor warned me there would be triggers that would happen throughout life and it was a matter of working through these. Over the following months I had moments where I repeatedly questioned my self-worth. Am I worth anything? This was the thought that was travelling through my mind. The saying from chapter four kept constantly reverberating:

Spot the girl…

To keep out the question

"Without it, is she worth anything at all?"

It took some time to claw my way back following my coffee with Lee; although, it was a little easier than previously. I have been reassured this was quite a normal emotion to go through these times of regression; but it did take me longer to work through than I expected.

Sometime later, when these emotions got the better of me, I sent Lee a brief email. I was not feeling myself and needed some clarification. This resulted in a phone call from Lee explaining his reasoning for not looking at me which were valid, as I did have a nasty virus.

I felt much better for not only raising my concerns but also talking it out. Following this, I had a good night's sleep.

Upon reflection I was still traversing the effects of the past year, getting to know myself, my various emotions, and thoughts again. Conceivably this is easier said than done when you still haven't the strength to think with clarity, which I feel was the state I was in.

Learnings for me were not to take things too personally, but nonetheless to let others know, in a gentle way how their actions affect me. To move forward, and to let it go.

I reviewed my book and took some of my own advice and went for a massage. Again, the trauma was hiding in different muscles. I'd gone for the massage to relieve the tensions in my neck, and especially my shoulders. Yet it was in my back that I needed to relieve the tension, I was always on guard, so to speak, needing to be prepared, protective; these emotions were hiding in my spine. The work performed on my back enabled me to come away with a revitalised outlook.

It was time for me to refocus; I had lost my way. As mentioned previously, I used to plan out three months at a time the things I wanted to achieve, but leaving this flexible for anything that came my way. It was a rough guideline. I set about forming my new goals for the next three months, with the potential for other goals after that. A six-month outlook, you might say. This provides me with focus, but also reinforces 'Yes', I am worth something to someone somewhere and so are you.

The Red Rose Foundation Queensland's mission statement is 'change the ending'. I am pleased to say I have changed the ending, and the ending continues to change as I continue upon this journey. Smiling along the way.

The truth is, healing doesn't mean the damage never existed. Healing means the damage no longer controls you. A woman is like a tea bag, you never know how strong the tea will be until it's in hot water. Think about it.

There might be parts of this book that make you feel like you want to take back what is rightfully yours. If this is the case, then do it, believe in yourself. Your inner self. Reclaim what is rightfully yours. Learn to use your voice. Use your inner strength and trust yourself.

People will judge you as they no doubt will judge me. I cannot stop that, none of us can. It is what I choose to think and do that matters, and I choose to move forward, laughing, smiling and to enjoy my new journey in life.

Always enjoy the conversations you have with anyone, especially family and friends. They are ALL precious.

I am a Domestic Violence <u>survivor</u> and I have changed the ending.

ACKNOWLEDGEMENTS

This book is dedicated to my children and any person who wants to leave, is in the process of leaving, and may find my personal experience of domestic relationship escape helpful.

I extend a huge, 'Thank you!' to Dani for sharing all the lovely encouraging captions which started my scrap book. Thank you for taking me out to lunch once a fortnight and helping me acclimatise to being in the world again. I socialised and gained the courage to go out for coffee, visit the library, the boathouse, and many other places—these outings helped me gain confidence.

Kai, my baby boy, what a rock you are! Thank you for your constant phone calls to check in on me, for your help whenever I needed it, for being there. I love you and thank you from the bottom of my heart.

Renee, thank you for being present on the end of the phone, and able to make me laugh when I needed distraction from events that made me anxious. You provided such a great time on my holiday break that took me back to my roots. You helped me through my knee operation, and so much more. I am grateful.

To all the girls from the Red Rose Foundation Qld, without your help and support I would not be here today. As the Red Rose Foundation mission statement says, I have changed the ending, and remarkably, this constantly changes and provides me with excitement and purpose in life. Thank you, to all of you for your support.

To my brother, thank you, for providing accommodation in my time of need. This allowed me the solitude and freedom to reflect, which enabled me to bring this book together.

To my family, my friends and relatives, thank you all for supporting and guiding me through what I can only describe as an interesting yet emotional journey.

Bubbles, for forever being there for me.

Marg, for your advice, help and direction.

To Mum and Rikki, I feel you with me, guiding and providing me with strength, thank you.

And my sincere thanks to Leanda, for your guidance, honesty, support and ability to be able to "hear" my voice. You have assisted me to tighten and brighten my story, to encapsulate and convey all that I wanted to say, which has been invaluable. I am so grateful, thank you.

REFERENCES

1 Red Rose Foundation Queensland: provide domestic violence services https://www.redrosefoundation.com.au/

2 Meaning of Shame / Google ND: Oxford Languages

https://www.google.com/search?q=shame+synonym&rlz=1C1GCEA_enAU1027AU1027&oq=shame+s&gs_lcrp=EgZjaHJvbWUqCggBEAAYsQMYgAQyBggAEEUYOTIKCAEQABixAxiABDIKCAIQLhjUAhiABDIKCAMQLhjUAhiABDIHCAQQABiABDIHCAUQLhiABDIHCAYQABiABDIHCAcQLhiABDIHCAgQABiABDIHCAkQABiABNIBCjEyMDk3ajBqMTWoAgiwAgE&sourceid=chrome&ie=UTF-8

3 10 Apr 2011 – 14 Mar 2024 Australian Women's Timeline. A timeline resource for teachers and students that includes major political, education, legal and social milestones for Australian women.

https://timeline.awava.org.au/timeline

4 Australian Institute of Strangulation Prevention.

5 Women's Legal Service, Non-Lethal Strangulation Webinar, Red Rose Foundation – Mar 22, 2019

https://strangulationprevention.com.au/

https://www.redrosefoundation.com.au/

https://www.youtube.com/watch?v=L8l-irHKXAU

6 Non-lethal strangulation definition. The Red Rose Foundation Queensland – Mar 22, 2019

https://strangulationprevention.com.au/domestic-violence-strangulation-webinar/

7 Google: 2024: Coercive Control

https://www.google.com/search?q=coercive+control&rlz=1C1GCEA_enAU1027AU1027&oq=coercive+control&gs_lcrp=EgZjaHJvbWUyDAgAEEUYORixAxiABDIOCAEQRRgnGDsYgAQYigUyBwgCEAAYgAQyBwgDEAAYgAQyCggEEAAYsQMYgAQyBwgFEAAYgAQyBwgGEAAYgAQyBwgHEAAYgAQyBwgIEAAYgAQyBwgJEAAYgATSAQk1OTkzajBqMTWoAgiwAgE&sourceid=chrome&ie=UTF-8

Google The Standing Council of Attorneys-General released the National Principles to Address Coercive Control in Family and Domestic Violence on 22 September 2023.

https://www.ag.gov.au/families-and-marriage/families/family-violence/coercive-control#:~:text=Coercive%20control%20involves%20perpetrators%20using,or%20a%20combination%20of%20both

Google 2024 Women's Aid Federation of England

https://www.womensaid.org.uk/information-support/what-is-domestic-abuse/coercive-control/#:~:text=Taking%20control%20over%20aspects%20of,Humiliating%2C%20degrading%20or%20dehumanising%20you

8 Google: February 13, 2024: Narcissist:

https://www.webmd.com/mental-health/narcissistic-personality-disorder#:~:text=It's%20human%20nature%20to%20be,and%20having%20narcissistic%20personality%20disorder

9 Google: ND: Trauma: Merriam-Webster
https://www.merriam-webster.com/dictionary/trauma

Google: ND: Emotions:

https://www.merriam-webster.com/dictionary/emotions

10 Emily Francis in her book 'The Body Heals Itself':

'The muscles simply store what the body has endured throughout this life – this is both great memories as well as traumatic memories.'

Emily Francis and Rev. Ashli Callaway, MDiv.

'Forgiveness is the practice of remembering a painful event, accepting that it happened as it did, and letting go of any attachment to the pain it caused.' It is not forgetting, condoning, tolerating, enabling or self-sacrificing.

11 Window of tolerance – National Institute for the Clinical Application of Behavioral Medicine:

https://www.nicabm.com/trauma-how-to-help-your-clients-understand-their-window-of-tolerance.

12 Google: Jun: 2024:

https://www.stylecraze.com/articles/hurt-quotes/

"The pain of yesterday is the strength of today." – Paulo Coelho

13 *Intimacy: Living Courageously* by Joyce Meyer

14 Google ND: Myers & Briggs:

https://www.truity.com/test/type-finder-personality-test-new.

15   Report: Name: Published Sharman Douglas Fitzgerald.pdf
Description: Published version.

https://minerva-access.unimelb.edu.au/items/1a1335b9-6935-5cd6-a9b8-e1890c58a2ac/full

Report Title: Review of domestic violence deaths involving non-fatal strangulation in Queensland. Date 2021 – Leah Sharman, University of Queensland; Heather Douglas, University of Melbourne; Robin Fitzgerald, University of Queensland. University of Melbourne website:

16   Stephen Martin and Joseph Marks Messengers

17   Carroll Izard at the University of Delaware analytically outlined 12 discrete emotions:

18   Google: ND: Oxford Languages: Trust

https://www.google.com/search?q=trust+meaning&sca_esv=a5295d27d6bcdf79&rlz=1C1GCEA_enAU1027AU1027&sxsrf=ADLYWIKVD7Gpy8EHTn_gbN5ahcE4OdMbvA%3A1719892829438&ei=XXuDZrGuGq3l2roPzd6tqAk&oq=trust+synonyms&gs_lp=Egxnd.3Mtd2l6LXNlcnAiDnRydXN0IHN5bm9ueW1zKgIIBTIKEAAYsAMY1gQYRzIKEAAYsAMY1gQYRzIKEAAYsAMY1gQYRzIKEAAYsAMY1gQYRzIKEAAYsAMY1gQYRzIKEAAYsAMY1gQYRzIKEAAYsAMY1gQYRzIKEAAYsAMY1gQYRzINEAAYgAQYsAMYQxiKBTINEAAYgAQYsAMYQxiKBUidUFAAWABwAngBkAEAmAEAoAEAqgEAuAEByAEAmAICoAINmAMAiAYBkAYKkgcBMqAHAA&sclient=gws-wiz-serp

Google: 31 Jan 2023: Being vulnerable

https://www.google.com/search?q=vunerable&rlz=1C1GCEA_enAU1027AU1027&oq=vunerable&gs_lcrp=EgZjaHJvbWUyBggAEEUYOTIMCAEQABgKGLEDGIAEMgwIAhAAGAoYsQMYgAQyDAgDEAAYChixAxiABDIJCAQQABgKGIAEMgwIBRAAGAoYsQMYgAQyCQgGEAAYChiABDIJCAcQABgKGIAEMgkIC

BAAGAoYgAQyCQgJEAAYChiABNIBCTYwMzZqMGoxNagCCLACAQ&sourceid=chrome&ie=UTF-8

19 Google: ND: mindfulness

https://www.healthdirect.gov.au/mindfulness#:~:text=Mindfulness%20is%20a%20mental%20state,with%20difficult%20emotions%20and%20situations

20 Google: 10 Mar 2016: When one door closes, another opens.

https://www.google.com/search?q=who+wrote+one+door+closes+and+another+opens&rlz=1C1GCEA_enAU1027AU1027&sxsrf=APwXEdf882iYTIdKL7Ysz8OxVu2muUArrg%3A1682566969724&ei=Oe9JZInpK4av2roPz7sj&ved=0ahUKEwjJ6am0ksn-AhWGl1YBHc_dCAAQ4dUDCA8&uact=5&oq=who+wrote+one+door+closes+and+another+opens&gs_lcp=Cgxnd3Mtd2l6LXNlcnAQAzIFCCEQoAEyCAghEBYQHhAdMggIIRAWEB4QHTIICCEQFhAeEB0yCAghEBYQHhAdMggIIRAWEB4QHTIICCEQFhAeEB0yCAghEBYQHhAdMggIIRAWEB4QHTIICCEQFhAeEB06BwgjELADECc6CggAEEcQ1gQQsAM6CAgAEIoFEJECOgUIABCABDoHCAAQgAQQCjoKCCEQFhAeEA8QHToECCEQFToHCCEQoAEQCkoECEEYAFC3C1iWRWCYSWgBcAF4AIABswSIAeNbkgEKMi01LjE5LjguMZgBAKABAcgBCcABAQ&sclient=gws-wiz-serp

21 The Art of Happiness a Handbook for living – His Holiness the Dalai Lama and Howard C Cutler.

'It takes inner strength to remain firm in our resolve, don't view tolerance or patience is a sign of weakness, it's not.'

22 Robert Louis Stevenson

'Make the most of the best and the least of the worst'

23 Google 16 Nov 2023

https://www.google.com/search?q=how+many+days+to+break+a+habit&rlz=1C1GCEA_enAU1027AU1027&oq=how+many+days+to+break+a+habit&gs_lcrp=EgZjaHJvbWUqBwgAEAAYgAQyBwgAEAAYgAQyBwgBEAAYgAQyBwgCEAAYgAQyBwgDEAAYgAQyDQgEEAAYhgMYgAQYigUyDQgFEAAYhgMYgAQYigUyDQgGEAAYhgMYgAQYigUyCggHEAAYgAQYogTSAQoxMDQ0NGowajE1qAIIsAIB&sourceid=chrome&ie=UTF-8

  24 Google: Nov 2023: knee replacement source

https://www.google.com/search?q=subchondral+oedema+knee&rlz=1C1GCEA_enAU1027AU1027&oq=subchondral+oed&aqs=chrome.1.0i512l2j69i57j0i512l5j0i22i30l2.19231j1j15&sourceid=chrome&ie=UTF-8

  26 Anthony Grant PhD and Jane Greene

'It's Your Life, what are you going to do with it?'

  27 Google: 2019: The Australian Institute of Health and Welfare (AIHW) an independent statutory Australian Government agency with more than 30 years of experience working with health and welfare data.

https://www.missionaustralia.com.au/domestic-and-family-violence-statistics

Domestic and family violence in Australia statistics

1. Women are more likely to experience abuse at the hands of a partner

1,2,3,4 AIHW (2019): Family, domestic and sexual violence in Australia: continuing the national story 2019. Canberra: AIHW

  28 Rebecca Dennis – 'Breathe'

29   Lynda Field – *Fast Track to Happiness*

31   Google: Publication/Start date 2021-11-08

https://espace.library.uq.edu.au/view/UQ:5da8771

Report: Review of domestic violence deaths involving fatal or non-fatal strangulation in Queensland

Sharman, Leah, Douglas, Heather, and Fitzgerald, Robin (2021). Review of domestic violence deaths involving fatal or non-fatal strangulation in Queensland. Brisbane, QLD, Australia: The University of Melbourne/The University of Queensland.

First published June 4, 2019

Google: Jess Hill – *See What You Made Me Do*; first published June 2019

https://www.jesshill.net/home/see-what-you-made-me-do/

32   Google: 19 Oct 2022: nature vs nurture essential biological factor, in addition to nurturing yourself through reflection of your life experiences.

https://www.google.com/search?q=nature+vs+nurture&rlz=1C1GCEA_enAU1027AU1027&oq=nature&aqs=chrome.2.69i57j0i131i433i512j0i433i512j0i512j46i131i175i199i433i512j0i433i512j0i131i433i512j0i433i512j46i131i199i340i433i465i512j0i131i433i512.4610j0j15&sourceid=chrome&ie=UTF-8)

33   Jules Evans Philosophy for Life.

35   Google: ND: larimar stone meaning

https://www.google.com/search?q=larimar+stone+meaning&sca_esv=a5295d27d6bcdf79&rlz=1C1GCEA_enAU1027AU1027&sxsrf=A

DLYWIIVwUVUSQ2yjiuXarxfFcb0S6Ncug%3A1719898329844&ei=2ZCDZqOjM-XL0-kPq4C-uA4&oq=lariAm+stone&gs_lp=Egxnd3Mtd2l6LXNlcnAiDGxhcmlBbSBzdG9uZSoCCAIyBxAjGLACGCcyBxAjGLACGCcyBxAjGLACGCcyBxAAGIAEGA0yBxAAGIAEGA0yBxAAGIAEGA0yBxAAGIAEGA0yBxAAGIAEGA0yBxAAGIAEGA0yBxAAGIAEGA1I3OEBULFlWL6KAXACeAGQAQCYAeIBoAHFBqoBBTAuMi4yuAEByAEA-AEBmAIGoALhBsICBxAjGLADGCfCAgoQABiwAxjWBBhHwgINEAAYgAQYsAMYQxiKBZgDAIgGAZAGCpIHBTIuMS4zoAeuMA&sclient=gws-wiz-serp

36 Google: March 2021:

https://search.abs.gov.au/s/search.html?collection=abs-search&form=simple&query=domestic+violence+deaths

https://www.who.int/news-room/fact-sheets/detail/violence-against-women

37 Google: Apr 2024: Examples of Resilience

https://www.google.com/search?q=resilliance&sca_esv=334a9bda33585e15&rlz=1C1GCEA_enAU1027AU1027&sxsrf=ADLYWIInLVtsOxxRe7jkQ7Y1DfvTl9lD8w%3A1719551290548&ei=OkV-ZqySIYLDjuMPgvWK0Ak&ved=0ahUKEwisl-Lew_2GAxWCoWMGHYK6ApoQ4dUDCBA&uact=5&oq=resil-liance&gs_lp=Egxnd3Mtd2l6LXNlcnAiC3Jlc2lsbGlhbmNlMgcQIxixAhgnMgcQIxixAhgnMhcQLhiABBi-RAhixAxjHARiKBRiOBRivATIKEAAYgAQYxiKBTIKEAAYgAQYxiKBTIKEAAYgAQYxiKBTIQEC4YgAQYxwEYChiOBRivATIHEAAYgAQYCjIHEAAYgAQYCjIHE-AAYgAQYCkj2JVAAWNMgcAV4AJABAJgB7wKgAYINq

LITTLE BITES

gE-FMi00LjK4AQPIAQD4AQGYAgugArINwgIKECMYgAQYJxiKBcICDxAjGIAEGCcYigUYRhj5AcICCxAAGIAEGJECGIoFwgINEAAYgAYsQMYQxiKBcICJxAAGIAE-GIoFGEYY-QEYlwUYjAUY3QQYRhj5ARj0Axj1Axj2A9gBAcICERAuGIAEGLEDG-McBGI4FGK8BwgIOEC4YgAQYxwEYjgUYrwHCAgUQABiABMICF-BAuGIAEGLEDGNQCGMcBGI4FGK8BwgITEC4YgAQYsQMYxwEYChiOBRi-vAcICFhAuGIAEGLEDGNQCGMcBGAoYjgUYrwHCAg4QABiABBiRAhixAxiKBZgDALoGBgg-BEAEYE5IHBzUuMC40LjKgB5NQ&sclient=gws-wiz-serp

ABOUT THE AUTHOR

Bobbin has a deep appreciation for life itself. From a fortunate upbringing with loving parents she fondly recalls a childhood full of wonder and exploration that undoubtedly set firm foundations for her love of nature and understanding of the spirit world.

Only when married, did she face the opposite and the unthinkable.

Drawing on her background of quality control and compliance in the service industries sector, with a keen eye for detail and organisational skills, Bobbin took all she had learned to provide herself with the quality of life she'd once known.

Following her escape from Domestic Violence Bobbin has resumed her passion and appreciation for nature where she is an active member of her local community garden, continuing to honour her passion for helping others.